Alternative Approaches to Education

This book is designed to give parents and teachers information on the alternative education options available in the UK. It covers three main areas:

- **Outside the state system**: Small schools; Steiner Waldorf schools; Montessori schools; democratic schools and schools with other alternative philosophies.
- **Doing it yourself**: Setting up a small school or learning centre; educating at home; flexible schooling.
- **Alternatives within the state system**: how some state schools are finding different ways of working.

The values, philosophies and methods of each alternative are described, along with the first-hand experiences of children, teachers and parents. There are answers to common questions and useful sources of further information.

This accessible and informative book is the ideal introduction for parents deciding how best to educate their children. It will also be of interest to teachers looking to build on their knowledge of different education philosophies.

Fiona Carnie is an education consultant and parent. For over ten years she has been working for Human Scale Education where she is involved in encouraging new initiatives in education in the alternative and maintained sectors.

Alternative Approaches to Education

A guide for parents and teachers

Fiona Carnie

RoutledgeFalmer
Taylor & Francis Group

LONDON AND NEW YORK

First published 2003
by RoutledgeFalmer
11 New Fetter Lane, London EC4P 4EE

Simultaneously published in the USA and Canada
by RoutledgeFalmer
29 West 35th Street, New York, NY 10001

RoutledgeFalmer is an imprint of the Taylor & Francis Group

© 2003 Fiona Carnie

Typeset in Bembo by
Keystroke, Jacaranda Lodge, Wolverhampton
Printed and bound in Great Britain by
TJ International Ltd, Padstow, Cornwall

British Library Cataloguing in Publication Data
A catalogue record for this book is available
from the British Library

Library of Congress Cataloging in Publication Data
A catalog record for this book has been requested.

ISBN 0–415–24817–5

Contents

List of figures   vii
Acknowledgements   ix

Introduction   1

PART I
Alternative approaches to education   **7**

1 Education – what for?   9

2 Small alternative schools *already here*   15

3 Steiner Waldorf education   42

4 Montessori education   71

5 Democratic schools   89

6 Other philosophies, other schools   99

PART 2
Doing it yourself   **115**

7 Setting up a small school or learning centre   117

8 Home-based education   132

9 Flexible schooling   150

PART 3
Alternative approaches in the state system   159

10   State schools: alternative ways of working   161

11   Small is beautiful: lessons from America   175

12   Parents as change agents   185

      Conclusion   189

      Index   193

Figures

1.1 Students at Settle School   13
2.1 The Small School at Hartland   16
2.2 Learning from the world   22
3.1 Steiner believed that we need to use our hands
     productively   43
3.2 Music plays an important part in Steiner education   46
4.1 Using Montessori's materials   73
5.1 Summerhill School takes a vote   91
6.1 Time for reflection   108
8.1 Home-educated children learning the glockenspiel   135
10.1 A school student council meeting at Cotham School   165

Acknowledgements

I would like to thank the many people who gave me help, encouragement and support while I was writing this book.

I am indebted to teachers, parents and students at the various schools who returned questionnaires, answered questions and wrote of their own experiences. Those who work in alternative schools deserve a special mention because of the energy, love and imagination that they bring to their work. Invariably they receive meagre remuneration but their commitment to a more holistic and child centred way of educating carries them through. Without them this book certainly could not have been written.

Particular thanks are due to Kevin Avison, Jenny Brain, Amanda Lake, Celia Lowe, Liz Snow and Caroline Walker for help that they have given. Roland Meighan has allowed me to use some of the quotes he collected in his *Freethinker's Guide to the Educational Universe* (Nottingham: Educational Heretics Press 1994) and I appreciate this very much. I am grateful to Barbara Isaacs and John Thomson for reading and commenting on draft chapters. I would like to thank my editor, Anna Clarkson, for her faith in this book and for her help and encouragement. My sister, Jennie Orchard, has given me endless advice and support which has been invaluable.

And I am eternally grateful to my husband Jamie for his insightful comments, and to our children Indigo, Kir and Saffron who have had to put up with an absentee mother, but who did so without complaint.

Finally I would like to thank Mary Tasker who read and commented on the text. She has been a wonderful friend and mentor and is a continuing source of inspiration.

Introduction

New learning technologies mean that we have no need to herd children in classrooms. New understanding about how the brain functions will force us to rethink what we think we know about learning. We are witnessing the last days of a 19th century education system.

Sir Christopher Ball, Chancellor, University of Derby

What is education for? Is it about lighting a fire or filling a bucket? Is it about personal development or providing fodder for the economic markets? Is it about keeping children off the streets or instilling in them the knowledge, skills and attitudes to create a fairer and more sustainable world? Or is it a combination of all of these? Such questions should be at the forefront of any debate about schools because the way in which children experience education is a major factor in influencing how they live their lives and, by extension, the kind of society they help to create for the future.

The institution of school as we know it today was developed to educate the masses for work in an industrial society and has scarcely altered to take account of changing times. Teachers teach, children are expected to learn and packaged information is 'delivered' from one to the other.

But society has altered dramatically since mass schooling was invented in the nineteenth century, and the world is a very different place. Technological advances have brought huge changes to the nature of work and children leaving school today require a very different set of skills than they needed early last century. Consequently a different approach to education is needed, one which helps young people to find meaning and purpose in their lives and which will enable them to be active participants in society.

Growing numbers of parents, teachers and academics agree that our current model of schooling is outdated and that a radical rethink is needed. The legal requirement to teach a narrow National Curriculum, the emphasis on formal learning methods and the continuing existence of large classes make it difficult for schools to meet the educational and developmental needs of many children. It is increasingly recognised that children learn best in situations in which their individual needs can be taken into account, but it is difficult for teachers to do this within the present system.

Research into how the brain works and how people learn points to the need for wide-ranging changes. A major finding is that we all learn in different ways and at different paces, so a 'one size fits all' approach is unlikely to meet the needs of most children most of the time.

Furthermore, this is the information age – information is easily available from computers, books, television, radio and videos. The emphasis now needs to switch from 'cramming' facts to learning how to learn and how to apply what has been learned so that it can be used in different situations. There is the potential for education to be transformed by new technologies. Access to information and the ease of communication mean that children no longer need to spend five whole days each week at school, sitting in classes. A much more personalised approach is now possible.

Such views have precipitated a surge of interest in alternative approaches. Thousands of families are looking for different ways to educate their children as discontent with mainstream schooling rises. Home-based education, family learning centres and small parent and teacher-run schools – catering for primary and secondary children – are springing up all over the UK. Interest in more established alternatives such as Steiner and Montessori continues to grow. All of these are examples of models of learning which aim to tailor the educational experience to suit the child. There is a feeling amongst the parents and teachers involved that they are at the vanguard of a new educational era – an era in which education will be fundamentally redefined.

So what is alternative education? It means different things to different people and is consequently a term that is difficult to pin down. By definition it is about challenging mainstream educational ideology and offering something different, but that is not sufficient. The term is generally used to refer to approaches that are based around the needs of the individual learner. My own view is that a truly alternative approach is holistic, in that it aims to develop the whole person and is underpinned by ecological values.

In practice, what all the projects mentioned in this book have in common is first that they are small enough for teachers and students to know each other well, thereby creating a sense of community to which people feel as though they belong. All members of the learning community are respected and cared for. Second, because teachers know their students individually they can respond to their needs and interests and develop a learning programme which is meaningful and relevant for each. Third, learning in these projects is rooted in experience. It is an active and participatory process whereby children, through exploration, discussion and collaboration, convert information into knowledge.

There are now over seventy alternative schools in the UK; more than 20,000 children are being educated out of school and these numbers are rising. The number of alternative schools is higher in many European countries, where governments are committed to providing and funding a range of schools so that parents can choose an education which suits their child. In America, parents and local communities can design new schools according to what they believe will benefit children educationally and these schools will receive public funding. In the UK we are lagging behind because public funding for such educational ventures is rarely available. As a result, most alternative schools need to charge fees, thereby making themselves inaccessible to the majority of children.

Some state schools are grappling with the question of how to bring schools into the twenty-first century but are constrained by the tight grip on education that is exerted by the government. This has now extended beyond what is taught in schools to encompass teaching methods. Teacher training institutions which traditionally included courses on child development and educational philosophy are now mainly concerned with teaching trainee teachers how to deliver the National Curriculum. State schools are thus caught in a trap. Even if they want to develop new methodologies they will be increasingly hard pushed to find teachers who have enough understanding of education theory to be able to work in new ways.

The aim of this book is to introduce some of the alternative educational approaches that are available in the UK and further afield to a wider public in order to raise awareness of different kinds of schooling.

The main criterion for inclusion is that the school or project, in one way or another, is challenging old orthodoxies. The word education comes from the Latin *educare*, meaning 'to draw out'. The alternatives in this book put the child at the centre of the educational process, seeking to provide learning experiences which help each one to develop and grow. Each project challenges (or belongs to an organisation which challenges) the notion that education is merely about the receipt of knowledge. The concern is more with education for personal and social transformation.

Having said this, it is not always completely clear-cut. A number of the schools which are included do teach the National Curriculum or parts of it for a variety of reasons. There may be pressure from some of the parents, or the schools themselves may consider that children moving on to other schools need to be prepared. There may be pressure from the UK Office for Standards in Education (OFSTED) which is responsible for inspecting these schools and which insists that they offer a broad and balanced curriculum. As far as secondary schools are concerned, GCSE's are based on the National Curriculum and so schools offering these exams will inevitably cover the same ground. Alternative schools want to survive and in order to do this they have to be responsive to the wishes of parents. However, the prevailing ethos at each one relates first and foremost to meeting the needs of the children.

Faith schools have not been included, with one or two exceptions. Most teach the National Curriculum as well as instructing children in a particular faith which has been chosen by the parents. The *raison d'être* of most (but not all) alternative schools is, by contrast, about encouraging children to make up their own minds. They therefore teach children *about* different faiths and festivals but do not, as a school, subscribe to any one in particular.

The first Part of the book introduces a range of alternative educational philosophies. Each chapter ends with a list of schools in the UK where these philosophies are put into practice. Part 2 advises parents on how to go about providing an alternative for their child in cases where there is none in their area, by setting up a school or learning centre, educating at home, or combining conventional school with home-based education in a flexitime approach. Part 3 concerns state education, giving examples of some alternative ways of working both here and in the US. Chapter 12 suggests how parents can work together to bring about change.

Further reading

Carnie, F., Large, M. and Tasker, M. (eds) (1996) *Freeing Education*, Stroud: Hawthorn Press.

Gatto, J. (1992) *Dumbing us Down*, Philadelphia: New Society.
O'Sullivan, E. (1999) *Transformative Learning: Educational Vision for the 21st Century*, London: Zed Books.

Notes

The schools included in this book responded to a questionnaire. Where there are inconsistencies in the information between schools it is because this is what the schools themselves provided.

1   The list is not exhaustive as alternative schools tend to come and go. If you know of any that are not included, please email carnie@clara.co.uk
2   Details about each school are correct at the time of going to press but are inevitably subject to change. Up-to-date information can be obtained by contacting the school.
3   Throughout the book personal pronouns have been avoided wherever possible. In cases where it has been unavoidable a teacher is referred to as he whilst a pupil is referred to as she.

Part I

Alternative approaches to education

Chapter 1

Education – what for?

Dear Teacher

I am a survivor of a concentration camp. My eyes saw what no man should witness: gas chambers built by learned engineers, children poisoned by educated physicians, infants killed by trained nurses, women and babies burned by high school and college graduates. So I am suspicious of education.

My request is: help your students become human. Your efforts must never produce learned monsters, skilled psychopaths, educated Eichmanns. Reading, writing and arithmetic are important only if they serve to make our children more human.

Anonymous

Successive governments, concerned about the underachievement of British children and the detrimental effect of this underachievement on the economy, have been determined to raise academic standards in education. This aim has underpinned changes to the state education system since the early 1980s, in particular the introduction of the National Curriculum with its associated tests and the school league tables.

In the midst of the flurry of change that has characterised school life over this period, two crucial questions seem to have been ignored by policymakers. First, are the kinds of changes that have been introduced in the best interests of children? and second, what is education for anyway?

In answer to the first question, many educationalists believe that a narrow and prescriptive National Curriculum has not suited all children, with the result that many young people have been marginalised. Teachers, constrained by an overloaded curriculum and with little spare class time, have found it difficult to respond to children's interests, the outcome has been that many have lost interest in learning. In the past teachers could make time for a child who brought a fascinating object into the classroom, or a teenager who brought an interesting if tangential question into a discussion, by diverting the lesson to follow up these threads of interest. These threads often brought moments of real illumination. Teachers today have little time for such diversions, and lessons can often seem irrelevant to children.

There is a comprehensible rationale to teaching children in inner city Newcastle the same material at the same time as children in rural Devon. It allows children to transfer more easily from one school to another if their parents move and enables the authorities to measure children's learning and compare schools. However, if this rigidity prevents teachers from rooting the learning experience in children's lives it is counterproductive. The curriculum has to have meaning for children if they are to be able to engage with it, and it is the connection with their own lives that imbues it with such meaning. A curriculum that is devoid of meaning to children will inevitably affect their motivation to learn. And an unmotivated child is a difficult, if not impossible, child to teach.

Primary aged children have seen 'non-essential' (and non-tested) activities such as sport, music, drama, environmental projects and school trips considerably reduced. Children as young as five or six spend a large part of their day sitting at a table when what they need most are activity, hands-on experiences, participation, collaboration and play. Older children at primary school and secondary school pupils spend much of their time passively receiving 'knowledge' in preparation for National Curriculum tests.

Recent studies have found that British children are among the most tested in the world. The tests show what most good teachers know anyway and only measure a narrow set of skills. They do not show whether a child is caring and compassionate, innovative and creative or good at working collaboratively with others. They do not indicate whether a child is happy and confident with a secure sense of self. They do not register if a child is a brilliant musician, environmentalist or computer genius. Yet these attributes are as important if not more so in determining the extent to which the child will live a fulfilling and productive life. Teachers forced to concentrate on teaching narrow academic skills for tests are compelled to underplay the significance of other fundamental aspects of a child's education.

It is clear to many that the tests are not carried out for the benefit of children but rather to enable the government to measure the performance of schools. Children are being subjected to the stresses of repeated testing in order that the government can assess – and demonstrate to the electorate – the extent to which it is meeting its targets. Their other purpose is to give parents a blunt instrument by which to judge the effectiveness of local schools. Sadly, many parents have accepted this mechanistic view of education and have been persuaded that the tests are beneficial to children.

The results of the tests, collated annually into national league tables, have served to set school against school regardless of their differing situations and widely varying intakes. Schools which were already perceived as good have become hugely oversubscribed whereas schools in challenging circumstances have often seen their rolls, and consequently their budgets, fall. An inequitable system has become even more inequitable creating considerable dissatisfaction amongst parents, many of whom have been unable to get children into the school of their choice.

It can be argued that none of these developments – the National Curriculum, the tests or the league tables – were conceived with the interests of children in mind, but rather for political ends. Their effect on children and on the attitudes of young people towards education have, in many cases, been mostly negative. Asked what they think of school, the majority of children say that it is boring. What an unbelievable waste of childhood. What an inexcusable waste of resources. If one aim of education is to encourage a love of learning, on this count alone, the system is utterly failing many children.

As a society we cannot afford to turn young people off education. They are the future. The government is right in saying that the quality of the future depends heavily on the quality of our education system. But this begs the second question – what is education for? What kind of future is envisaged?

At the time of writing, in the wake of the 11 September New York disaster, the question has a particular poignancy. Is education about enabling those living in rich countries to create more of the same, thereby reinforcing an inequitable world system of western prosperity and Third World poverty? If so, we are likely to see many more such atrocities as people from countries exploited by the West for their natural resources or their cheap labour vent their anger and desperation at our profligacy. If instead, through education, we instil in young people the values, attitudes and skills to create a fairer and more sustainable world then this can be the beginning of a new world order in which the inequities are gradually ironed out and in which east and west, north and south can coexist peacefully. Nothing less than this is a reasonable goal of our education system.

It is no longer good enough to feed young people information and knowledge which bolster up the global divide. Science, history, economics and food technology taught without reference to ethics are barren. Instead of imparting knowledge in a vacuum we must find ways of showing children the power of that knowledge by drawing out the connections between subjects and how they relate to the real world. If, through their lessons, young people explore the responsibilities of farmers, drug companies, the oil industry, supermarkets and clothing manufacturers they are more likely to leave school understanding that they too have responsibilities as members of a global community; understanding that each one of their actions – putting on their clothes, eating a hamburger, getting in a car and going shopping – has an effect on others in different parts of the world and involves a moral choice on their part. If children learn to connect with these issues at school by analysing, questioning, debating and using their minds to delve beneath the surface then there is a chance of shaping a better world. There is a chance that young people will realise that through their work and the way in which they live their lives each one can make a positive contribution.

How can this shift in what and how children learn be implemented? How can schools incorporate this moral dimension so that children are challenged personally to think critically and to make choices?

It is difficult for children to engage with global issues until they have some understanding of local issues. Their own experiences must therefore be the starting point. The key questions are 'how do members of the school community treat each other?' and 'how does the school community as a whole take care of the world?' In answering these questions schools must find ways to become truly equitable, inclusive and environmentally sustainable communities. In short each one must become a microcosm of how we want the world to be. If these questions are addressed by schools then there is a better chance that they will be addressed by society as a whole.

To become an equitable community entails giving every child, teacher and parent a voice and ensuring that every voice is heard and every voice counts. Children need to be involved in decisions about their learning and assessment as well as in decisions about how their school is run. Parents need to be given the opportunity to participate in discussions and decisions about issues which are of concern to them. Teachers and schools need the autonomy to develop methods and approaches which are appropriate to their students and their own local situation.

Schools will only become truly inclusive communities by valuing and caring for every one of their members – adults as well as children. By focusing on the importance of relationships, by making sure that each child and their family is known, by giving all teachers a pastoral responsibility that is integrated with their academic role, schools can ensure that every child feels secure and supported. This is no small task but it is only by taking relationships seriously and by valuing all members of the school community regardless of race, colour, creed, appearance or sexuality that schools will be able to say that they are truly inclusive.

If they are to become environmentally sustainable communities, schools must ensure that their ethos, curriculum, policies and practice are integrated. They need to resolve the contradictions between teaching children the need for sustainability while practising wasteful and unsustainable policies within the school. Teaching children the reasons for global warming goes hand in hand with a school transport policy that puts bikes before cars and an energy policy that includes insulating the school and buying energy from renewable resources. In this way, children learn that change is possible.

Figure 1.1 Students at Settle School learning about their environment.
Credit: Jane Thomas

The emphasis needs to be on the word community – on creating schools where all people have a sense of belonging and can actively contribute so that education is a dynamic, meaningful and relevant process. This is the challenge for schools in the twenty-first century.

It is an interest in these perennial questions about education that has led many people, in the UK and further afield, to set up educational alternatives. These projects take many different forms but perhaps one thing is a constant: the recognition that human beings do best in situations in which they are known, cared for, supported and valued; in short where they are part of a community. The different kinds of alternatives which are available in the UK are explored in the following chapters.

Further reading

Clark, D. (1996) *Schools as Learning Communities*, London: Cassell.

Jeffs, T. (1998) *Henry Morris: Village Colleges, Community Education and the Ideal Order*, Nottingham: Educational Heretics Press.

Miller, R. (ed.) (2001) *Creating Learning Communities*, Vermont: Foundation for Educational Renewal.

Orr, D. (1994) *Earth in Mind: On Education, Environment and the Human Prospect*, Washington: Island Press.

Richardson, R. and Wood, A. (2000) *Inclusive Schools: Inclusive Society*, London: Trentham Books.

Sterling, S. (2001) *Sustainable Education: Revisioning Learning and Change*, Totnes: Green Books.

Chapter 2

Small alternative schools

> British schools are too big, too much subject to state control and lack the values that we need for a healthy society.
>
> Satish Kumar, 'Liberating education', *Resurgence* 1991

The Small School, Hartland

In the early 1980s, a group of parents decided to set up a small secondary school in the village of Hartland in North Devon. These parents did not want to send their children on the two-hour round trip to the nearest comprehensive school, thereby making them start the life of a commuter at the age of 11. They felt it was inappropriate for the children, who had been brought up in a rural community, to suddenly find themselves at a huge school with more students than there were people living in their village. They wanted the children to have an education which related to and drew on their local community and environment – and they wanted to be involved.

A building in the village was bought, teachers were hired, money was raised and the first Small School was launched. It was no ordinary school, however. It was the beginning of a movement in education, which has grown steadily over the last two decades.

Children and teachers at the Small School are on first name terms; there is no uniform and students, parents and teachers all have a say in how the school is run. The children take it in turns to cook lunch and clean the school. The emphasis is on educating the whole person – head, hand and heart.

Alongside academic studies, children learn practical skills such as building, making clothes and growing vegetables – skills that will be useful throughout their lives. There is a strong focus on developing each

Figure 2.1 The Small School at Hartland.
Credit: The Small School

child's creative potential through music, drama, art and a wide range of different crafts. There are special weeks in the second half of the summer term when the normal timetable is suspended. Instead, each of these weeks is devoted to a different activity in which the whole school participates: storytelling for example, or building a solar shower, African drumming or a camping expedition. On one occasion a French week was organised during which students learned about different aspects of French life, culture, history and geography. The week culminated in the preparation of an authentic French meal for families and friends of the school. One year the whole school visited Japan, performing a Shakespeare play in a number of different towns and villages.

Children at the Small School do a maximum of seven GCSE's (many do five – which is sufficient for university entrance) and this enables the school to offer a much more rounded education than the majority of British schools. It does not mean that the children study fewer subjects, rather that learning is not dominated by exams. Most academic work is done in the morning leaving afternoons free for sport, drama, art and other activities. Because classes are small and children are motivated much more can be achieved in each lesson than in a conventional school.

The approach to learning is also different. When children work together in small groups there can be greater emphasis on discussion and collaboration. Learning is related to children's own experiences, and the role of the teacher is not to deliver information but rather to build on these experiences to help the child towards greater understanding.

The philosophy of the school is underpinned by environmental values and it aims to educate children to help create a more sustainable future. This philosophy impacts upon all aspects of school life, from decisions about energy consumption and the building materials used in the school to the content of the curriculum. School lunches consist of organic, locally grown and locally purchased food. What this means is that in their everyday life at school children are not just learning about environmental sustainability but are practising it too.

As with all good things there is a significant down side. The school has to raise all its own funds which it does in a variety of ways including voluntary contributions from parents, grants from charitable trusts, a guardian scheme and a non-stop, year-round programme of fund-raising events. It does not receive a penny from public funds. It has been told that it is too small to offer a broad and balanced curriculum and that small schools are too expensive to run (even though it spends no more per capita than the LEA-funded secondary schools in the area). In spite of this it turns out well balanced, thinking and caring young people. Its exam results are good – some years it has been top of the league tables in Devon – and many ex-students go on to university. It has no truancy, no exclusions and children like going there.

Human scale education

Such was the interest shown nationally and internationally when the Small School started that the charity Human Scale Education was set up in order to promote more widely the values that were in action at the school. Human Scale Education believes that smallness of scale helps to create the interpersonal relationships that enable children and young people to become confident and resourceful individuals, capable of respecting and caring for each other and for the environment. The charity's motto, 'Education as if people matter', is taken from E. F. Schumacher's *Small is Beautiful – Economics as if People Matter*. Human Scale Education advises groups of parents and teachers wishing to set up their own community school, gives support to existing small schools and encourages schools in the maintained sector to find ways of working in smaller units. Member schools subscribe in varying degrees to Human Scale Education's philosophy, which holds that education should comprise a number of essential elements all of which depend on small structures to be put into practice. These elements – positive relationships, a holistic approach to learning, democratic participation, involvement of parents and the wider community and a commitment to a fairer and more sustainable world – are discussed in more detail below.

Positive relationships

Good relationships are at the heart of a successful school. Teachers need to know their pupils well if they are to be able to teach them effectively. They need to know about their interests, their strengths and weaknesses and to understand where the child is in terms of progress. With this knowledge and understanding of their pupils, teachers are able to tailor the learning to suit each child.

The importance of good relationships goes beyond the relationship between the teacher and the child to the whole community of the school. In a community built on trust and openness, where teachers, pupils and parents show respect and care for each other, children feel secure and can develop the self-confidence and self-esteem which make learning and personal growth possible. When children are drawn into meaningful relationships with their teachers and other adults they are better able to see them as real people and this affects their whole attitude to school and to learning. In such an environment teachers feel valued and supported. Parents feel included and as a consequence are more likely to contribute to the life of the school and the learning of their children. All members of the school community feel as though they belong and have a commitment to the school.

A holistic approach to learning

Education is about developing the whole child and should therefore aim to foster creative, emotional, moral and spiritual growth as well as intellectual development. Prioritising music, art, dance, drama and a range of crafts helps children learn to express themselves; by encouraging moral and emotional development they learn to live with each other in a positive way. Spiritual awareness is developed by providing the kinds of experiences which help children to know and understand themselves. Such a broad and holistic approach to education is more likely to produce rounded and balanced individuals than one which focuses almost exclusively on academic achievement.

To help children make sense of the world it is important to draw out the connections between subjects rather than to concentrate on their differences. A curriculum based on topics or themes that are grounded in academic disciplines but which relate to each other, to real world issues and to children's own lives, will have more meaning than a subject-based approach. The learning experience needs to be active and interactive as children learn more through discussion, experiment and hands-on project work than by passively receiving information. By bringing the subject matter to life in this way children can make it their own and are more likely to be able to apply what they have learned in other situations.

Democratic participation

Involving children with teachers and parents in decisions about their learning and about school policy is an effective way of increasing motivation and commitment, but the rationale goes beyond this. If we want children to be active participants in society then the process of learning to make decisions and take responsibility for those decisions must start at school. Mistakes will be made, there will be bad decisions; but people learn from their mistakes and this is an important process. It is a way of helping young people to understand how they can have an effect on their world and bring about change. In most schools children are told what to learn, what to wear and how to behave. In a sense teachers are even told what and how to teach. It is a disempowering experience for all concerned. Anyone who is involved in the life of the school and who will be affected by decisions should have a voice. There is much talk about teaching children citizenship, but as with many things, the best way to learn about it is to do it.

Partnership with parents and the local community

Schools are strengthened by the involvement of parents and the local community, as this widens the responsibility for children's education. Many parents want to have a close relationship with their child's school and to be involved in his or her learning, but schools have often found it difficult to facilitate this, with the consequence that parents can feel left on the outside.

Parental involvement is a key factor in raising attainment, because teachers and parents can work together in support of the child. There are a host of ways in which to involve parents in the life of the school – through discussion groups, involvement in decision-making, by drawing on parents' skills – and these can all bring many positive benefits.

The relationship with the local community is also important. A school is not an isolated institution; it affects and is affected by the locality in which it is situated. There is much to be gained both by encouraging local people to become involved in the school and contributing to local life by sharing school facilities and resources, and by undertaking social and environmental projects in the community. The boundaries between the two need to be collapsed so that the school is an integral part of the community and the community is part of the school.

Environmental sustainability

If, as a society, we take seriously the challenge to create a fairer and more sustainable world then the work of schools must be underpinned by environmentally sustainable principles. It is not enough for children to learn about global warming, the depletion of natural resources or the problems of soil erosion if the school's own practices do not reflect an awareness of these issues and a commitment to addressing them within the daily life of the school. How many schools have the heating turned up and the windows open? How many schools do not even recycle their waste paper and cans? And how many schools serve up mass-produced, unhealthy food bought through large chains rather than produced locally? We cannot expect children to care about these issues unless the school as a whole is prepared to take them seriously.

Decisions about the building, its heating system, insulation and lighting as well as the furniture, materials and resources used within the school should all be informed by the principles of environmental sustainability. So too must the content of the curriculum. Some schools have carried out an environmental audit or a food audit so that they are able to gauge the impact of their institution on the earth. Such activities offer the potential for cross-curricular learning, drawing, as they do, on a range of subjects. They also help to relate the learning process to children's own lives. By making young people aware of the consequences of their actions in this way they are encouraging them to make informed decisions and this is surely a core purpose of education.

Small structures

It is not smallness per se that is important, for there can be bad small schools; it is what smallness or a human scale makes possible that counts. Many adults find large settings intimidating, and yet most children have to contend with large numbers on a daily basis. How can a child be known and responded to as an individual in a class of thirty? How can teachers begin to teach thirty children all of whom have different interests, are at different levels, who progress at different speeds and who learn in different ways? How can a child feel a sense of belonging in a 1000-strong institution where it is not even possible to know the names of all the other people there? Businesses are increasingly organising their staff in sections or teams and schools too need to be of a size so that children, teachers and parents can feel a sense of community.

For Human Scale Education size is the key issue, because smaller structures make it possible to put into practice the principles outlined above. The charity is not suggesting that all schools can be small schools but rather that all schools should find ways of organising themselves so that children can have a 'human scale' experience.

Other small schools

The Small School at Hartland, embodying these principles, has been the model for a number of schools which have been set up since. Some are rural, some are urban; some are secondary, some primary and some span both age ranges; some take a percentage of children who are deemed to have special educational needs, some are set up entirely for such children. Some have as few as six children; some have sixty. Each school is different depending on the priorities of the founders.

Dame Catherine Harpur's School in Ticknall, Derbyshire has worked hard to involve parents closely in all aspects of school life. There is a focus on encouraging children to become independent learners. Park School in Dartington, Devon emphasises creativity and environmental values. Educare Small School in Kingston, Surrey focuses on the emotional and spiritual development of children. Priors School in Priors Marston, Warwickshire was opened as a small, community-run independent school after the local education authority closed down the village school which had been in existence since 1847. The will to open Dame Catherine's came from parents; Educare was founded by a teacher with a vision; the pressure for Priors School to reopen came from the local community. Some of these schools are highly innovative in their

Figure 2.2 Learning from the world.
Credit: Park School

approach, others keep a close eye on the National Curriculum and even administer the SATs. Each is an expression of the community it serves.

To open such a school is not an easy task. Funds have to be raised, buildings found, teachers employed. It is a time- and energy-consuming process (described in Chapter 6) which is fraught with difficulties; but each one of the groups which has succeeded has been driven on by a belief that what is provided by the state is sorely lacking.

The biggest problem for these schools is that the majority receive no public funding. This means that they lead a precarious existence and over the years many have been forced to close. A number of the schools ask parents for voluntary contributions. Others charge fees because it puts them on a more stable footing. Human Scale Education is pressing for public funding, believing that they should be non-fee paying so that they are open to all children regardless of their parents' ability to pay. Until such time as the government gives financial support to parents and teachers wishing to set up their own schools they will continue to struggle, and their effectiveness will be compromised by the disproportionate amount of time and effort which has to be spent on fund-raising in order to survive.

Questions often asked about small schools

In such a small school, how will my child make friends when there are so few children her own age?
What generally happens in small schools is that children make friends with older and younger children as well as children of their own age. It is unnatural for children only to mix with others in their year group and children benefit from relationships with others who are different ages. In a small community, the onus is on children to all get on with each other.

How do children manage when they leave a small school to go on to other schools or college?
In most cases they seem to manage remarkably well. Generally speaking, the self-confidence which they have developed whilst at the school stands them in good stead for coping with changes and new situations. Older children who have moved on to college already know how to learn independently and have often found their peers, who are enjoying their first taste of freedom, relatively immature by comparison.

What if you can't afford to make a financial contribution to the school?
Some small schools charge fees which are non-negotiable and so if you cannot afford them you will not be able to send your child. Others have bursaries available. Some schools ask for a voluntary contribution and if you cannot afford to make a financial commitment, they may accept payment in kind – home grown vegetables for example or help with transport. Alternatively, you may be able to offer your time doing some teaching, classroom assistance or administrative work.

List of schools

South East

> Abinger Hammer Village School
> Hackhurst Lane, Abinger Hammer, Dorking, Surrey RH5 6SE
> Tel: 01306 730343

School established: 1982 after LEA school closed

Age range of pupils: 2½ – 8

Maximum number of pupils: 20

Number of staff: 1 plus volunteer assistance

Curriculum: The curriculum is as broad as possible and makes use of the rural surroundings. Since most pupils move on to state schools, it is based on the National Curriculum but extends beyond this, often concentrating on different aspects in different terms. Extra-curricular clubs are offered.

Description: The school in its present form replaced the County First School in 1982 after an unsuccessful fight to avoid the closure of a maintained school. It is based on the conviction that young children benefit from attending a small, local school. The whole community is involved in fund-raising and in all kinds of practical support.

The children meet the pupils of another small local school (Peaslake) on a regular basis, and take part in the local music festival each year. The teacher arranges and supervises several after-school clubs, some with topics chosen by the children.

As well as serving the children of Abinger Hammer, Abinger Hammer Village School can offer an alternative to local parents from other villages. This option is often welcomed by those with a diffident or school-shy child, who can soon gain confidence and enjoy learning in a happy 'family' atmosphere.

Educare Small School
12 Cowleaze Road, Kingston upon Thames, Surrey KT2 6DZ
Tel: 0208 547 0144   Fax: 0208 546 5901
Email: Educaresmallschool@btinternet.com
Website: www.educaresmallschool.org.uk

School established: 1997

Age range of pupils: 3–11

Maximum number of pupils: 50

Number of staff: 4 full time, 4 part time

Curriculum: National Curriculum with lots of art, drama and music, Alexander Technique and simple meditation.

Description: The school is based on the belief that if children are able to deal confidently and skilfully with each new step in their life they will grow into independent, fulfilled adults able to take an active part in the society of the future. It is concerned with the holistic development of each child. Children are encouraged to learn and develop at their own pace. The school works in partnership with parents and everyone's contribution is welcomed.

A parent's view
We discovered Educare by chance, relocating to Kingston on Thames two weeks before the summer holidays and with a 3½-year-old who would need some sort of nursery stimulation in the autumn. We still remember the dismal trawl through the various private and state schools that were prepared to see us: a prep-school head who barked at my talk-a-lot-and-run around (and suddenly bemused) son 'we only like sit-down-and-work little boys here'. A state school which allowed a visit but 'strictly without your children, because they might disrupt the school day or the parents' chat with the head, and if, in the end, there is no place for them, they will be disappointed'. Educare presented itself as a few lines on a LEA handout as an approved provider of nursery care and anecdotal evidence from a friend of a friend that it was 'near the station and nice'. We had no expectations.

   From the moment we approached Educare's playground with its funky multicoloured wall, planted tyre mound and thatched play frame my son was shouting at the gate to be allowed in and his just-walking brother was having a bash at freeing himself from the buggy. The buzz of happy children playing outdoors in the sunshine, every teacher willing to chat to the visitors (big and small), train set retrieved from cupboard to be vetted and approved by the (very exacting) prospective pupil. Added to this, busy classroom walls, reward stickers emblazoned on the children's chests ('Jamie, what a lovely kind boy you are' 'Fabby-dabby leaf painting, Poppy'), no raised voices and kindergarten staff with little ones on hips and holding hands. No wonder my son said immediately on leaving 'I really want to go to that school where everyone used my name'. That's just what we wanted for him too.

A few years later, and the baby in the buggy is now enjoying the same playground, teachers and train set that were chosen for him by his brother. It hasn't been all plain sailing, our first child definitely found a rebellious and attention-seeking streak, faced with being part of a class for the first time. Staff levels are such that he received a lot of the individual attention that he demanded and also was taught (gently and without any knocks to his self-esteem) how to respect the needs of the group. Our concerns when he was behaviourally difficult were always addressed and discussed. Everyone, from the Head down, had time to talk to us, to make suggestions, to sympathise and never, ever to blame us or him. We find the mix of ages in the older class, and the access that younger children have to the older peer group who are taught in the same space, perfect for the needs of our very bright little boy.

Our younger son, in contrast to his brother, is less intellectually mature and very shy, finding difficulty making eye contact and initially even talking to adults from outside his family. The gentle and inspired help that he has received in the Kindergarten, where he is now one of the eldest children, has transformed our timid, grumpy caterpillar into a chatty, fun-loving, friend-loving, eye-contacting butterfly!

We do not know what kind of paths our children are going to follow in the future, and where their personalities and intellectual abilities will lead them. We are confident, however, that they will have both had the finest of possible starts to their education, both in the three R's and life skills at Educare Small School.

Elizabeth Lawrence

Lewes New School
Talbot Terrace, Lewes BN7 2DS
Tel: 01273 477074   Fax: 01273 483054
Email: office@lewesnewschool.co.uk

School established: 2000

Age range of pupils: 2½–11

Maximum number of pupils : 80

Number of staff: 3 teachers, 3 part time assistants

Curriculum: National Curriculum used as a framework. Creativity at the core of the curriculum in all subject areas. Project work and cross-curricular themes.

Description: The school aims to bring excitement and adventure back into learning. There is a learner-centred approach using the National Curriculum as its starting point. Staff design the curriculum from the children's interests. Work is organised around themes that allow children to learn a variety of skills and gain knowledge and understanding of their world. Children, parents and teachers are involved as active participants in the creation of the school community in which every individual counts.

Willow House
19 Downs Side, Sutton SM2 7EH
Tel: 0208 643 7277
Email: rvm@zoom.co.uk

School established: 2001

Age range of pupils: 5–11

Maximum number of pupils: 8

Curriculum: National Curriculum subjects tailored to the needs of each child.

Description: The school provides a learning environment for children whose needs are not fully met within a mainstream school. Some children attend part time.

South West

Little Arthur Independent School
St Martin's, Isles of Scilly, Cornwall TR25 0QI
Tel: 01720 422457

School established: 1997

Age range of pupils: 7–18

Maximum number of pupils: 10

Number of staff: 2 plus specialists when necessary

Curriculum: National Curriculum maths, English and science plus ecology, gardening, agriculture, crafts, history, geography, accounting and island sports.

Description: Little Arthur was set up to give island children an island education in which subjects like agriculture, ecology, accounting and real crafts and skills (boatbuilding, spinning, metalwork and building) are given priority. Works cooperatively with other small schools and home educators by providing a home-educator pack in National Curriculum maths, science and English and a range of IGCSE (International GCSE) subjects and by offering craft skills and/or study weeks for individuals or small groups.

Park School
Park Road, Dartington, Totnes, Devon TQ9 6EF
Tel: 01803 864588 Fax: 01803 868533

School established: 1986

Age range of pupils: 3–11

Maximum number of pupils: 60

Number of staff: 8

Curriculum: Emphasis on the teaching of maths and English, environmental education and creative arts. Importance is also attached to children's social and emotional development.

Description: Park School provides a human scale and holistic education. It is now in its fifteenth year of providing progressive education in spacious and beautiful surroundings on the Dartington Hall Estate. Along with the teaching of basic skills, the school fosters children's creativity and environmental awareness and builds self-esteem and self awareness. Teaching is in small groups with well qualified staff. Parents play an important role and are active contributors to this innovative school.

On being a Park School parent

I never intended sending my child to a private school. Having worked in the state system all my life, I had always felt ideologically, if not always emotionally, wedded to it. However, for various reasons, I wanted my child to attend early years education at the age of four and that was not available in Devon within the state system. My choice at that time was between a very rigid, formal, pre-preparatory school where I saw children dressed in uniform and standing in rows reciting their tables – and Park School. When I asked how long I could stay with my son at the pre-preparatory school as a 'settling in' period I was told, 'Oh no, we find children settle in much more quickly if parents do not stay at all'. I was told at Park School that I could stay as long as I or my son wanted me to. My decision was made. That alone told me so much about those two schools.

Benedict did, in fact, settle in to Park School Nursery very quickly. I stayed with him for the whole of his first day and we both had a wonderful time. His dad stayed with him for his second day. And on the third day I said goodbye, and waited for the phone call. It never came – and when I picked him up at 3 pm he was pleased to see me, but did not want to leave.

I told myself he could transfer into the state system when he was five. I told myself the same thing again when he was seven. Now – six-and-a-half years – twenty terms – later, I am dreading him leaving this July to go to secondary school.

I could not possibly do justice – in a few words – to everything that has been good about Park School for us. Every member of staff, every encounter, every child deserves mention and to single out any would be doing a huge injustice to the rest. Perhaps it is better just to describe the totality, the atmosphere, the ethos.

When you walk into a classroom at Park, children do not stand up and say, 'Good Morning', or 'Good Afternoon' in unison. Most of them are far too interested in whatever they are doing at the time even to notice that the door has opened. Those who do notice are likely to rush over and to show you their latest invention, project, or piece of art work with enormous enthusiasm and pride.

It is this huge enthusiasm for learning, and pride in themselves, their own creativity and their potential that children gain from an education at Park. Every child is valued equally, for who he or she is and will become – not for what they do – or do not do. Every child has freedom to explore what he or she wishes to explore. The opportunities are enormous. My own son has been on three residentials; he has been on local trips to nature reserves; he has been on all-day adventures in an open twelve-person canoe; he has been to the theatre, to the cinema, to literature festival events, to art galleries; he has a Danish penfriend whom we are looking forward to welcoming to our home next term; he plays the piano, the violin, the cello and has achieved excellent results in Associated Board examinations; he has learnt to play the Balinese gamelan with many other children with whom he toured the West Country playing in the BBC Millennium Music Festival.

From an early age, Benedict's passion has been natural history and environmental science. He couldn't have been better catered for at Park. From the goldfish and the guinea pigs when he was in the nursery to the numerous chickens and two Vietnamese pot-bellied pigs which all children help to care for, he has learned to love and have a deep respect for all life. The children cultivate their own garden – flowers, herbs and vegetables – and have the opportunity to cook their own produce.

As far as academic achievements are concerned, because he has never been pressurised to read, write, compute, etc. such 'work' has never been much of an issue at home. But just as, earlier in his life, he gradually, naturally and confidently began to talk, walk and run, so I have been aware of his emerging ability and wish to devour increasingly sophisticated fiction and non-fiction at enormous speed, to grapple with ever more complicated mathematical concepts and to help me with my IT problems. It just happened.

Georgina Weaver, parent, Park School

The School in the Woods
1 Upper Mount Pleasant, Freshford, Bath BA2 7UG
Tel: 01225 722597

School established: 2001

Age range of pupils: 5–8

Maximum number of pupils: 10

Number of staff: 5

Curriculum: Emphasis on nature and learning with the seasons. Academic subjects covered also wide range of arts and crafts, organic gardening and ecology.

Description: The aim of the school is to be a place where children love to learn and where they are active and creative partners in the learning situation. Children have played a role in drawing up the school's programme.

The Small School
Fore Street, Hartland, Bideford, Devon EX39 6AB
Tel: 01237 441672
Email: smallschool@ukgateway.net

School established: 1982

Age range of pupils: 11–16

Maximum number of pupils: 40

Number of staff: 4

Curriculum: Broad and balanced between creative, practical and academic activities.

Description: The school aims to teach the skills, knowledge and values necessary for the creation of a fairer and more sustainable future. Students contribute to their community by taking part in the cooking, gardening and cleaning. Parents contribute to the school by offering teaching or other skills. The school aims to be a resource for the local community and to use the community as a resource. For example, students participate in local environmental conservation projects. The local focus is balanced by a global perspective; links with schools in other countries provide opportunities for travel and students study global issues as part of their humanities programme. A wide variety of optional activities provide students with different learning styles and a chance to achieve and value themselves. Close informal relationships between staff and students ensure attention to each student's needs.

The future of this school is currently under review.

Learning at The Small School, Hartland

I am a pupil at the Small School in North Devon. It is one of the original small schools and was founded by Satish Kumar.

I enjoy being part of the school and part of the wider family that is involved in it. For me it is very family orientated as my younger brother and sister are also students, my father teaches art and my mother cooks the lunch one day a week. I think that the more back-up you get from your parents the better your school work will be. My mum helps me with my homework and will check if I get it in on time, and because my teachers know that my mum is actively involved in my homework they will talk to her about it. If I am not doing it they know that she will back them up if they ask her to.

One of the features of the school that I find really important is the cooking. Four days a week one adult and two pupils cook and on one day a week the lunch is cooked by an older pupil with two younger ones. Each day the cooks plan the meal and do the shopping. They have to keep to the budget of 80p per person. The food is vegetarian. We are taught how to cook, about the importance of supporting local shops, the reasons for using mainly organic and locally produced goods and about composting left over food.

At lunch time all of the pupils and staff sit down together and say the Peace Prayer. This is one of the most important things that happens in the school because it mixes the teachers and pupils of all ages, and it shows people how to behave at a table. When lunch has been eaten the cooks wash the plates up and the cooks from the day before wipe the tables and sweep the floor.

Pupils at the Small School do their own cleaning too. This involves sweeping, hoovering, emptying bins and tidying up. This too is an important aspect of school life as it teaches us to clean up after ourselves. We keep the school cleaner during lessons and break because we know that if we make a mess we will have to clean it up later on.

Academic lessons are only held in the mornings. In the afternoons we are allowed to decide what we want to learn. The options include pottery, needlework, woodwork, photography, climbing and many other activities. These courses are run by parents, staff and members of the local community, all of whom are very committed and put a lot of energy into their lessons.

Having the freedom to decide what we are going to do in the afternoons is valuable because it gives us the responsibility to make sure that we do not waste our time. If a student has chosen to be in a lesson, they do not disrupt it because they have chosen to be there. If someone does attempt to disrupt the lesson the other students tell him or her to stop because they want to make the most of the time they have in that particular lesson.

At school the teachers are respected for the job that they do and for who they are. They earn this respect by showing respect to each pupil. Pupils need to respect each other as well. This happens and it helps to create a harmonious atmosphere to work in.

The school relies on the pupils' cooperation and illustrates that if you give students the freedom that they want, they have to take the responsibility that comes with it. If students do take that responsibility then it makes the school a place that is a better place for everyone to work in. I think that school should be a place that helps to teach people about freedom and responsibility as well as all of the other things that are taught.

Lucy Mellor, student, aged 15, The Small School, Hartland

Midlands

Dame Catherine Harpur's School
Rose Lane, Ticknall, Derbyshire DE73 1JW
Tel: 01332 862792

School established: 1987

Age range of pupils: 3–11

Maximum number of pupils: 45

Number of staff: 3

Curriculum: The content of the National Curriculum is drawn upon, as is the best material from other sources. Emphasis on an individual approach to learning means that formal literacy and numeracy hours are unnecessary but key skills are promoted in a variety of stimulating ways.

Description: Dame Catherine's is a rural school. There is the facility for three class groups, each not exceeding fifteen children, with a maximum of eight children in the nursery. The school borders open countryside on the outskirts of the village. Outside is a spacious playground, a large garden, including an activity area, dens and quiet areas and a wildlife pond.

The Head teacher's View
The school was originally founded by Dame Catherine Harpur in 1744. Under the terms of the trust the school buildings were bequeathed to the villagers of Ticknall and Calke to provide free education for the children of local people.

Over the years the school has adapted and evolved to meet the demands of the modern age. The main principles of the school are to provide an affordable alternative to the mainstream local authority schools, to create a small nurturing environment for children aged 3 through to 11, to free children from the pressures of attainment targets and testing and to work in class groups of no more than fifteen children. All this is made affordable through parental involvement. Parents gain credits towards the cost of their child's education by working in the school gift shop (sited at a nearby craft centre), voluntary work to maintain the day-to-day running of the school and through helping with fund-raising activities planned throughout the year. By keeping the school affordable a good social mix of children is achieved.

Perhaps the most challenging part of working in a school such as this is that since the team is very small, the pressures tend to fall on the head teacher. I teach full time so administrative work can pile up. Without my parent/secretary and the help of the cleaner and the parent caretaker I would sink under a constant stream of post, paperwork and phone calls. Plenty of humour is needed to carry us all through. I must say that the school management team, consisting of parents and friends of the school, also takes some of the stress and is very supportive.

I have been extremely encouraged by the generosity of the villagers and various organisations in the area who have donated gifts and money and included us in rural activities. I hope in the years to come the school can continue to put something back into the community.

Working in a school like this has many challenges. It can be professionally isolating. It can be difficult to be out of the mainstream because of the lack of contact with other agencies and local schools. We are small and have limitations as far as resources and accommodation are concerned. There never seems to be enough money or enough time. However the positive environment and family atmosphere are an added bonus as they are not so easy to achieve in other settings. I have enjoyed the relationships that you can achieve with the children in a small setting as this. Here's to many more challenging (but fun) years!

Margaret Whyte, head teacher, Dame Catherine Harpur's School

The Priors School
School Lane, Priors Marston, Rugby, Warwickshire CV23 8RR
Tel: 01327 260527
Email trustees@priorsschool.co.uk

School established: 1996

Age range of pupils: 3–11

Number of staff: 4 full time, 1 part time plus volunteers

Curriculum: National Curriculum as a basis plus French. Local people who have particular skills offer a range of extra subjects.

Description: A village school with a village ethos and a strong emphasis on community values.

Scotland

Scoraig Secondary School
Scoraig, Dundonnell, Wester Ross IV23 2RE
Tel: 01854 633381   Fax: 01854 633372
Email: stewart.mcphail@u.genie.co.uk

School established: 1988

Age range of pupils: 12–16

Number of staff: 2 plus volunteer teachers

Curriculum: As any mainstream school, but enhanced by the uniqueness of the situation so we can develop the individual's talents and interests and take part in more unusual activities.

Description: This school, in a remote setting, was established by parents but is funded by the local education authority.

Special needs schools

South East

Cave School
2 Rectory Grove, London SW4 0DZ
Tel: 0207 622 7186   Fax: 0207 498 5275
Email: CaveSkool@aol.com

School established: 1976

Age range of pupils: 14–16

Maximum number of pupils: 14

Number of staff: 3

Curriculum: Full time, broad curriculum leading to national qualifications – includes intensive personal support.

Description: At present ten places are funded for Lambeth pupils, four for referrals from other LEAs. The school is primarily for disaffected pupils, seven girls and seven boys with profound emotional difficulties. Personal and family support is offered in the context of development through learning.

> The Home School of Stoke Newington
> 46 Alkham Road, London N16 7AA
> Tel: 0208 806 6965

School established: 1994

Age range of pupils: 11–16

Maximum number of pupils: 16

Number of staff: 1 full time, 8 part time

Curriculum: National Curriculum to GCSE in seven subjects. French optional.

Description: Provides a stress-free learning environment for children who are school phobic, victims of bullying or who are dyslexic.

A parent's view

Small is beautiful: small is caring; small is supportive; small is exactly what we were looking for when our then twelve year old son began to struggle, academically and socially, at his mainstream comprehensive.

Like every other parent who is considering sending their child to the Home School we were offered a week's trial before deciding to take up a place. Our minds were made up after the first day when our son came home from school smiling and eager to return the next day. This was a heart-warming transformation from the anxious, worried and food-refusing boy we had become used to having around.

Our youngest son is very dyslexic but an otherwise fairly normal and intelligent teenager (if such a person exists!). The local comprehensive was unable to give him anything but minimal support to help him with his learning and to help him cope with the teasing that sometimes bordered on bullying. He was labelled as a 'no hoper', expected to be unable to achieve any examination success, but because he was well behaved and undemanding of attention, his problems were often ignored and we realised that the outlook was bleak for him. Our other two children had thrived on the hurly burly, busy social and academic life at the same school but this was not for our youngest son.

Thank goodness we had heard about the Home School and there was a place for him there. Although he still finds reading difficult he can get by, and to our great pleasure he succeeded in achieving five GCSE subjects (maths, double science, geography and art) at grades A–C and a distinction in the Certificate of Achievement in English. He has now moved on to studying theatre and television lighting and sound at a local FE college.

How did the Home School succeed where mainstream schooling failed? Well it is small, and consists of two classes so each student is treated as an individual with their own work programme in each subject. There is also the opportunity for regular one to one sessions with qualified and trained staff to help with specific problems. When I told my son I was writing this and asked him what he thought was the best thing about the Home School he thought it was because all the teachers know, understand and value the strengths of each child and use these strengths to work on the weaknesses.

Above all the Home School is small enough to care about each child. There is total commitment to ensuring each child achieves his or her full potential from the enthusiastic head teacher through to every single teacher and helper. The school offers a very safe environment for adolescents to grow and mature into confident and caring young people who are well on the way to achieving their goals in life.

Any disadvantages? Some parents may find the smallness, which for us was a great plus, may not suit their child. It is not cheap, but some local authorities will help with fees, and we certainly felt that any financial sacrifice was more than compensated for by the enthusiasm for learning that was reawakened in our son.

Judith Cattermole, parent, The Home School

East Anglia

St Andrew's School
Lower Common, East Runton, Norfolk NR27 9PG
Tel: 01263 511727   Fax: 01263 511727

School established: 1988

Age range of pupils: 6–12, and part time older pupils

Maximum number of pupils: 16

Number of staff: 8

Curriculum: Based on National Curriculum with special consideration for literacy, occupational therapy and language therapy.

Description: St Andrew's is a special school for pupils with communication difficulties including dyslexia, dyspraxia and Asperger's Syndrome. It is run on Quaker principles of non-violence and egalitarianism and aims to devise ways in which children with problems can receive an education suited to their needs, not necessarily involving full-time attendance at school. The school also acts as a part-time unit for those who attend other schools or are educated at home and need extra specialist help with some aspect of communication.

Teaching at St Andrew's School

St Andrew's is a small school for children with communication difficulties. Some children attend the school on a part-time basis, either combined with attendance at another school or with education at home, depending on parental preferences and the child's individual needs.

Despite the small numbers of full-time pupils the school always appears to be a hive of activity of both staff and children. The most striking thing that I have noticed as a relatively new member of the team was the relaxed and 'stress-free' atmosphere in the school. All children can talk freely about their learning difficulties or disabilities and are not made to feel socially unacceptable, as can often happen in mainstream schools. The children are usually tolerant of others and can accept them for what they are.

In a short period of time pupils become more confident in both their academic and personal development. Often these children have not coped in other schools and have lost confidence in themselves and their ability to learn. They often have very low self-esteem but, with a high adult–pupil ratio and specialist teaching, a positive educational environment is soon achieved.

On a day-to-day basis every child follows a basic skills programme set to cater for their individual academic needs in literacy and numeracy work. This is followed by work with literacy, listening skills, personal and social skills, language skills and therapy sessions. Again this is adapted for each individual child to suit his or her needs. Assessment is regularly made to see how each child is progressing and they each have their own achievement and target plan.

In the afternoon the school timetable follows more of a mainstream curriculum including humanities, art, music, PE, RE, rural studies, project work, drama and design and technology.

One of the main aims of St Andrew's School is to integrate a pupil back into mainstream education if possible. Again this is achieved at a pace which suits the individual child and with the full support of both schools.

Parental involvement within the school environment is also very much in evidence. This is particularly important with the pupils who are educated at home or partly at home and school. Both the parents and staff need to show a positive attitude so that the pupils can be encouraged to reach their full potential academically and socially.

Beverley Knott, teacher, St Andrew's School

Midlands

Bramingham Park Study Centre
Bramingham Park Church, Freeman Avenue, Luton, Bedfordshire
LU3 4BL
Tel/fax: 01582 494696
Email: bpsc@btconnect.com

School established: 1995

Age range of pupils: 11–16

Maximum number of pupils: 18

Curriculum: Based on National Curriculum but flexible approach to meet individual needs.

Other sources of funding: Some students funded by their schools or the LEA.

Description: This learning centre was established for school refusers, victims of bullying, long-term sick and fragile children. Students can attend part or full time.

St Paul's Community Foundation School
Hertford Street, Balsall Heath, Birmingham B12 8NJ
Tel: 0121 440 1349 Fax: 0121 440 8688
Email: anita.halliday@stpaulscom.co.uk
Website: webmaster@stpaulscom.co.uk

School established: 1972

Age range of pupils: 11–16

Maximum number of pupils: 60

Number of staff: 10

Curriculum: English, maths, art, design, drama, music, PE, home economics, childcare, community studies, information and communications technology.

Exams offered: GCSE, NVQ, various certificates (basic skills).

Description: The school was founded to work with pupils alienated from large mainstream schools and has an informal and supportive style and structures. There is lots of counselling and additional activities such as outdoor pursuits and field trips. The emphasis is on individual action plans and work-based learning in years 9–11 onwards.

North West

Oaktree Education Trust
24 Aigburth Drive, Sefton Park, Liverpool L17 4JH
Tel: 0151 727 7231   Fax: 0151 726 8988

School established: 1986

Age range of pupils: 11–16

Maximum number of pupils: 40

Number of staff: 5 full time, one part time

Curriculum: Key Stage 2 and 3 maths, English, science, a personal development programme, job skills, holistic lessons and project work linking in key skills, ICT, art, science, world studies.

Description: Oaktree Education Trust is a learning centre which provides a service to students in the Liverpool community who are either victims of bullying, or come from families where there is little value placed on the benefits of education, or have a history of being subjected to emotional, physical and sexual abuse or who have behavioural problems and have been excluded from numerous schools, but who do not pose a safety risk to other students.

For information

Human Scale Education
Unit 8
Fairseat Farm
Chew Stoke
Bristol
BS40 8XF
Tel: 01275 332516 Fax: 01275 332516
Email: info@hse.org.uk
Website: www.hse.org.uk

Further reading

Hodgetts, C. (1991) *Inventing a School*, Hartland: Resurgence.
Kumar, S. (1991) 'Liberating Education', *Resurgence*, 148: September/ October.
Schumacher, E. F. (1973) *Small is Beautiful: Economics as if People Matter*, London: Abacus.
Spencer, R. (1999) *Fifteen Small Schools*, Bath: Human Scale Education.

Chapter 3

Steiner Waldorf education

> It is of great importance to find an answer to the needs of our times
> through an education which is based on a real understanding of
> humankind's evolution.
>
> Rudolf Steiner

The Steiner Waldorf School movement comprises around 700 schools,
1500 kindergartens and 50 teacher training institutes around the world.
The movement dates from 1919 when Rudolf Steiner (1861–1925)
founded his first school in Stuttgart in Germany, called the *Waldorfschule*.
Since then schools based on his philosophy have been founded in
North and South America, Asia, Africa and all over Europe. In Britain
there are currently around thirty schools, forty-three kindergartens and
two teacher training courses.

Rudolf Steiner had many interests and wrote widely in fields as
diverse as biodynamic agriculture, anthroposophic medicine, architecture
and art, as well as education. His educational philosophy is child-centred
and based on his belief in the importance of childhood in determining
how we live our lives. Education is seen as a process of gradual awakening
or unfolding of the self. Each child is different and learns in different
ways, and one of the main challenges for schools is to respond to those
differences in a way that allows the child to become herself without
encouraging egotism. It is in our childhood years, Steiner believed,
that we develop our identity and the inner strength to deal with life's
challenges.

The purpose of education is to help the child make sense of the
world and this is achieved through a holistic approach. Steiner believed
that education comprised three main strands. It had to be practical,
artistic and develop the intellect. Developing a healthy relationship

with the natural world is a key element and a theme which recurs throughout.

The curriculum in all Steiner schools has a strong emphasis on practical skills and from an early age children are taught to knit, make clothes, cook, garden, do woodwork and metal work. Many of these skills are disappearing fast in our increasingly technological world. Not only do children need to be able to use their hands productively, but the experience of the nature of different materials teaches the child how the world is. Through these activities the child develops the power to think.

The artistic development of the child is encouraged through art, sculpture, music and drama, all of which permeate much of the learning that takes place on a daily basis. Children's work is generally beautifully coloured and decorated – a work of art in itself. Topics are often explored through storytelling, song or movement or in short plays. Children learn their tables by singing them or through movement. The alphabet is learned by taking the letter out of a picture which suggests the abstract shape; for example 'w' emerges out of the picture of a wave, 's' out of the picture of a snake.

In the development of intellectual skills young people learn to form their own views and values and to understand themselves and their place

Figure 3.1 Steiner believed that we need to use our hands productively.
Credit: Hereford Waldorf School

in the world. There is a strong focus on social skills and spiritual values in all Steiner schools. Steiner believed that it is important to enable the child to experience awe, reverence and devotion. Although a Christian ethos underlies the education its insistence on the universality of the spirit enables it to take root in Judaic, Buddhist, Islamic, Indian, Japanese and Chinese cultures.

Steiner's theory of child development underpins the educational practice in Steiner schools and is based on his observation of how a human being evolves physiologically, psychologically and spiritually. Childhood is divided into three distinct stages. What and how children learn at each stage is determined by their development.

The first stage covers the period from birth up to the age of six or seven. The middle years, sometimes called the heart of childhood, are from seven to fourteen and the third stage covers adolescence to emerging adulthood. In the early years the emphasis is on the development of the will. The middle years focus on the development of feeling and in older children, the development of thinking skills takes a central place in the curriculum.

The early years

Children start kindergarten at the age of three-and-a-half or four and stay until they are six. The emphasis in early years education is very firmly on play and on learning by doing. Steiner believed that children benefit from a long childhood and saw play as crucial in facilitating physical, social and emotional development. There is no reading, writing or maths at this stage, indeed no formal education at all, although preparation for maths and language skills takes place through everyday activities such as cooking and storytelling. It is considered damaging to the child to be pushed into formal learning too soon. Instead the emphasis is on learning through discovery. The children spend time painting, making, building, baking and other such practical activities. The play often involves imitating adults in their work and learning by example. Music, movement, drama, storytelling, nature activities and the celebration of festivals are an integral part of the day. The children learn songs, sometimes in foreign languages. Toys are simple and are generally made of wood and other natural materials. The idea behind the simplicity is that it leaves room for children to develop their imagination without all the detail being provided. No television is watched as it is believed that this interferes with the child's natural thinking processes.

These first years are seen as important in laying the foundations of the person. Kindergartens aim to provide a caring and home-like environment so that children can build up their confidence. There is a sense of freedom: the children are allowed to develop naturally without pressure whilst being given the care and help that they need.

The heart of childhood

In Steiner's philosophy of education children are thought to reach the next stage in their development at around the time when their second teeth appear. It is at this time, between the ages of six and seven, that they move on from kindergarten to begin more formal education. It is not until this stage that children are taught to write and then to read – in this order. Steiner believed that there was a change in consciousness at this age and that children begin to learn through pictures and images rather than just by doing and imitating. They live more in the realm of their feelings and this is reflected in the content and process of learning. Myths and historical stories often form the basis of learning during these middle years.

When the child joins the school in Class one the class is assigned a teacher who stays with the group for the next eight years. As a consequence the class becomes a tight social unit and deep relationships are formed. The teacher gets to know the children in his class extremely well and becomes a friend, guide and mentor rolled into one. It is the job of the teacher to create a curriculum which is appropriate to the group at each stage of their development. He is responsible for the main lesson each day, which is a two-hour period in the first half of the morning during which the main curriculum areas are covered in an integrated way through a succession of topics. The curriculum themes are carefully matched to the stages of the child's development. Topics are explored through action, art and thought and there is an emphasis on beauty. Children learning in this way understand the relationship and connections between the subject areas. The curriculum is like a spiral and classes come back to different subjects in different years, exploring them in greater depth, depending on the stage of development of the children. Computers are not used because it is considered that they stifle creativity, imagination and independence of thought.

After the main lesson each day the class is taught by different teachers for music, languages, craft and so on. Each teacher has a specialism and teaches classes other than his own in this subject area. Children thereby meet a variety of teachers. It is the responsibility of the class teacher however to oversee the development of each child in his class up to puberty, drawing together the many threads in their lives and preparing them for the next stage.

There is no competition between the children and they are not given marks for their work. Instead each receives the praise or help and support appropriate to her own situation.

Figure 3.2 Music plays an important part in Steiner education.

Credit: Edinburgh Steiner School

Adolescence

Children move into the Upper School at the age of fourteen. At this stage there is an increased emphasis on developing the young person's capacity for abstract thought. Teachers work with the idealism of adolescents to develop their questioning minds. The curriculum is designed to take account of the challenges of adolescence as the child's sense of self emerges. Young people's interest in relationships, their tendency to be critical of themselves and their questioning of the world around them are all harnessed in this stage of their learning. The aim is to help young people go out into the world as free, independent and creative beings.

The day begins with a main lesson, as in the middle years of schooling, but the difference is that these are now taught by subject specialists. A teacher takes a block of main lessons on a specific topic area every day for a block of three to four weeks after which a different specialist teacher takes over, starting a new topic. There are ten or eleven such teaching blocks per year. These are all interdependent and are not taught according to rigid subject disciplines. Alongside the main lesson there are regular classes in maths, English, a foreign language, religious education, science, sport, Eurythmy (a form of movement developed by Steiner) and craft. Each class has a guardian who is responsible for the pastoral care of the group and who coordinates the specialists working with his class.

General principles of Steiner schools

Schools are all co-educational and comprehensive; there is consequently a wide range of abilities and this is seen as important in children's social development. Each school is run by a College of Teachers which has overall responsibility for the school. There is no hierarchy and no head teacher. A Management Council on which parents are represented exists in an advisory capacity.

Schools adhere to a broad and internationally recognised curriculum. Children's progress is assessed by their teachers and there is no testing. Calculators and computers are not used in the early years as it is believed that an exaggerated emphasis on their use endangers the healthy development of cognitive and social skills. GCSE and A level examinations can be taken alongside the Steiner curriculum, though these exams are usually taken a year later than in state schools. This means that there is less associated stress and results are well above the national average.

All Steiner schools in the UK are currently fee-paying, although the movement is campaigning for public funding for its schools. Fees are kept as low as possible and in many schools are related to parental income. Where more than one child from a family attends a school there is often a significant reduction for the second child.

Questions often asked about Steiner Waldorf education

If a child has one teacher for eight years what happens if they don't get on?

This happens rarely but in cases where it does occur it is the responsibility of the teacher to try to understand the cause of the situation and to overcome it. As the class is taught by a number of teachers he can seek the advice of colleagues. There have been occasions where a child has been moved to a parallel class, or indeed been removed from the school altogether in cases where the parents have lost confidence in the teacher. More often than not the situation has been worked through successfully. The benefits of having a teacher who comes to know all the children in his class extremely well are considered to far outweigh any such difficulties.

Steiner developed an all-encompassing theory of education. Do all schools stick to this rigidly and what happens if there are aspects you disagree with?

Most Steiner schools in the UK are affiliated to the Steiner Waldorf Schools Fellowship and are thus committed to teaching the Steiner curriculum; but there is flexibility within this curriculum and schools interpret it in widely varying ways. Some stick closely to Steiner's teachings, others are freer in their interpretation. It is the responsibility of the teacher to create lessons appropriate to the developmental needs of his class. Just as all children are different, so too are all teachers and each interprets and teaches materials in his own way. If there are aspects of school life that the parents disagree with they can take this up with the teacher or with the College of Teachers but as with most schools, by agreeing to send your child you are implicitly accepting the philosophy and curriculum of the school.

How do children fare if they start at a Steiner school and then have to transfer to a state school or vice versa?
Sometimes children transferring from a Steiner school to a different kind of school can have difficulties initially as the whole method of educating is so different. Generally speaking they settle down well, their experiences at the Steiner school in awakening their interest and imagination standing them in good stead.

Children can move to a Steiner school at any age, though it is generally thought that the earlier this takes place, the better. Again the settling in process may take a while as expectations of the child may be very different, but if it is the right school for the child, she will soon learn to feel at home there. Having said this Steiner schools certainly do not suit all children, and close liaison between the family and the school is essential in making the best decision for the child.

List of schools

* Denotes schools which are members of the Steiner Waldorf Schools Fellowship.

South East

Alder Bridge School
Bridge House, Mill Lane, Padworth, Reading, Berkshire
RG7 4JU
Tel: 0118 9714471   Fax: 0709 2042631
Email: ABA@anth.org.uk   Website: www.anth.org.uk/ABA/

School established: 1993

Age range of pupils: 3½–12

Number of pupils on roll: 76

Number of staff: 5 full time, 5 part time

Curriculum: Steiner curriculum

Description: The school is in its eighth year as a lower school. It is located half way between Reading and Newbury on a semi-rural site by the Kennet and Avon canal. The main building is purpose built as a school with extensive grounds including an area of woodland.

Brighton Steiner School★
Roedean Road, Brighton, Sussex BN2 5RA
Tel: 01273 386300   Fax: 01273 386313
Email: bss1@talk21.com

School established: 1984

Age range of pupils: 3–16

Maximum number of pupils: 300

Number of staff: 35

Curriculum: Holistic education, teaches a wide range of subjects through an essentially artistic approach, following the development of the child. A wide range of other subjects from our own curriculum will also be studied up to age 16.

Description: A small, friendly Steiner school, surrounded by a strong community of parents, teachers and children who have worked hard over the years to bring it into being. The school is now expanding to take children up to age 16.

Michael Hall★
Kidbrooke Park, Forest Row, East Sussex RH18 5JA
Tel: 01342 822275   Fax: 01342 826593
Email: info@michaelhall.co.uk   Website: www.michaelhall.co.uk

School established: 1925

Age range of pupils: 0–19

Number of pupils on roll: 576

Curriculum: Steiner curriculum embodying cultural studies, sciences, general arts and humanities, crafts, music and movement and foreign languages. Art, music and drama are very important elements in school life. English as a foreign language is available during term time and the holidays.

Description: This is the oldest Steiner school in the English-speaking world and is situated in a rural setting in 50 acres on the edge of the Ashdown Forest, a mile from the village centre of Forest Row. It offers a broad education to boys and girls from birth to 19 including GCSE and A levels.

Perry Court School★
Garlinge Green, Chartham, Canterbury, Kent CT4 5RU
Tel: 01227 738285   Fax: 01227 731158
Email: perrycourt@ukonline.co.uk

School established: 1976

Age range of pupils: 3–18

Maximum number of pupils: 350

Number of staff: 36

Curriculum: Steiner curriculum

Ringwood Waldorf School★
Folly Farm Lane, Ashley, Ringwood, Hants BH24 2NN
Tel: 01425 472664   Fax: 01425 482442
Email: mail@ringwood-waldorf-school.fsnet.co.uk
Website: www.ringwood-waldorf-school.fsnet.co.uk

School established: 1974

Age range of pupils: 3–14

Maximum number of pupils: 300

Number of staff: 24

Curriculum: Steiner curriculum

St Paul's Steiner School
1 St Paul's Road, London N1 2QH
Tel: 0207 226 4454   Fax: 0207 226 2062
Email: info@stpauls-steiner-project.org.uk
Website: www.stpauls-steiner-project.org.uk

School established: 1995

Age range of pupils: 0–10

Maximum number of pupils: 150

Number of staff: 8

Curriculum: Steiner Curriculum

The School House
Carlton Hill, Brighton, Sussex BN2 2GW
Tel: 01273 602289

School established: 2001

Age range of pupils: 7–8 (to be extended)

Maximum number of pupils: 12

Curriculum: Steiner Curriculum

Description: This is a small, new school offering a homely, child–centred education.

South West

The Acorn School
Church Street, Nailsworth, Gloucestershire GL6 0BP
Tel: 01453 836508
Website: www.theacornschool.com

School established: 1991

Age range of pupils: 4–19

Maximum number of pupils: 100

Number of staff: 14

Curriculum: Steiner curriculum with academic curriculum in upper school. Also offers optional wood craft course in upper school.

Description: Small, co-educational school which offers a balanced education based on Steiner's principles. University entrance direct from school using school's unique modular programme. So far the school has a 100 per cent success rate in this respect.

The Meadow School
18–20 High Street, Bruton, Somerset BA10 0AA
Tel: 01749 813176   Fax: 01749 812177

School established: 1993

Age range of pupils: 2–12

Maximum number of pupils: 100

Number of staff: 10

South Devon Rudolf Steiner School★
Hood Manor, Dartington, Devon TQ9 6AB
Tel: 01803 762528   Fax: 01803 762528
Email: inquiries@steiner-south-devon.org
Website: steiner-south-devon.org

School established: 1981

Age range of pupils: 3–16

Maximum number of pupils: 350

Number of staff: 25

Curriculum: Steiner curriculum

Description: Situated in a rural area, close to Totnes. The seven acres of grounds offer many opportunities for sports, gardening and crafts.

Waldorf College Project
Centre for Science and Art, Lansdown Road, Stroud,
Gloucestershire GL5 1BB
Tel: 01453 840009 Fax: 01453 840010
Email: alasdair.gordon1@virgin.net
Website: waldorf-college-project.org.uk

School established: 2000

Age range of pupils: 16–19

Maximum number of pupils: 30

Number of staff: 1 full time, a number of part-time subject tutors

Curriculum: Two year programme covering a diverse range of thematic projects which integrate science and art. In the second year students also undertake a major individual project of their own choosing. Students create portfolios of their work. Weekly skills sessions include literacy, language, drama and crafts. There is a weekly review session where students make project presentations and attend co-management meetings.

Exams offered: No exams – continual assessment. Open College Network accreditation. Portfolio of project work.

Description: The College offers a dynamic education for young people developing:

• learning through experience and reflection
• freedom with responsibility
• creative thinking
• initiative
• self-motivation.

The college has a student co-management structure where students learn to problem solve, chair a meeting, plan study courses, review their work. This contributes to self-esteem and ownership of learning as skills in leadership, teamwork and communication are developed.

Wynstones School*
Church Lane, Whaddon, Gloucester GL4 0UF
Tel: 01452 429220   Fax: 01452 429221
Email: wynstones@ukonline.co.uk
Website: www.wynstones.org.uk

School established: 1937

Age range of pupils: 3–18

Maximum number of pupils: 300

Number of staff: 25 full time, 14 part time

Curriculum: Steiner curriculum

Description: Located in the countryside south of Gloucester. All pupils follow a varied core curriculum and can take GCSE and A level courses.

A parents' view

Steiner education is the greatest gift we feel we can give to our two boys aged 10 and 12. Both boys started school in the private system and then moved on to state schools when we relocated because of work. We discovered Steiner education three years ago and felt that our children were guiding us to this.

From the beginning they have been looked upon by everyone involved in their school as individuals and treated accordingly. They have consequently blossomed as pre-adolescents rather than shut down. This is as a result of their teachers' sensitivity to their personal differences and needs, embracing their soul, spirit and body. As their main teacher stays with them for eight years we as parents have built a wonderful and mutually supportive relationship with him. This carries all of us through the potential minefield of child rearing.

The teacher takes responsibility for building his class into a well-integrated social group and for being a mediator between the class and the world. He endeavours to bring the full reality of the world – both natural and social – to his pupils, relating it emotionally and intellectually to each stage of their development. Each subject is brought alive involving the students emotionally and practically, thus arousing interest and active participation. The natural rhythms of the earth are of key importance throughout their learning. The emphasis is on encouraging children to become creative and analytical in their own thinking processes rather than just to memorise facts. Instead of a competitive ethos children are constantly rewarded with praise and recognition for their own interest, connection and involvement with what is being studied.

Children come from a variety of different backgrounds and learn to respect each others' individuality, build relationships and work cooperatively. Our values at home are reflected within all aspects of their school life. The majority of fellow pupils do not watch television, have electronic games or use a computer yet and this pleases us. When friends come to stay they are polite, appreciative and, most importantly, they can *play*. Their inventiveness and imagination mean that there is no time to be bored and as they don't get homework until they get to teenage years, they visibly benefit from time after school, just to be, whatever their mood may bring. In many ways it is an old-fashioned childhood.

Both our boys adore school and cannot wait to see what treasures the day will bring, always inspired and excited by each new topic. They are fit, healthy and still pink-cheeked at the end of the day, week and especially as each term ends. Their inner spark of childhood is very much alive and extremely infectious. Their sense of wonder, gratitude and reverence has been cultivated and a connection between themselves and all that is out there in the world grows daily. We feel as parents that we are also on a journey and can honestly say that we are enjoying every minute.

Belinda and Andrew Montague, parents, Wynstones School

East Anglia

Cambridge Steiner School
24 Roseford Road, Cambridge CB4 2HD
Tel: 01223 516756
Email: info@cambridge-steiner-school.co.uk
Website: www.cambridge-steiner-school.co.uk

Age range of pupils: 3–7

Number of pupils on roll: 50

Curriculum: Steiner curriculum

Midlands

Elmfield Rudolf Steiner School*
Love Lane, Stourbridge, West Midlands DY8 1SB
Tel: 01384 394633   Fax: 01384 393608
Email: info@Elmfield.com
Website: www.elmfield.com

School established: 1946

Age range of pupils: 2–17

Maximum number of pupils: 330

Number of staff: 32

Curriculum: Steiner curriculum

Description: Situated on a green and leafy campus 13 miles west of Birmingham. Takes children up to GCSE. The mixed gender and ability classes each have twenty to twenty-five pupils. Facilities include a hall and gymnasium and specialised rooms for art, crafts and music. New buildings were opened in 1979 and 1995, providing additional class-rooms, a well-equipped science laboratory, a special hall for music, dance and movement, and facilities for information technology.

A student's view

I am sixteen years old and have been attending Steiner schools since the age of four. I started in the kindergarten in Edinburgh and then went on to Aberdeen for Classes one to four and finally in Class five I came to Elmfield where I am now studying for my GCSE's.

My earliest memories of school are of my first year in the kindergarten in the Autumn collecting chestnuts. I don't suppose I really started to think of school as somewhere where you worked until I entered Class one, aged six, and even then school was still about stories and play and it didn't really feel like work. At first I was a little slow learning to read as it didn't really interest me but when I did put the work in at the beginning of Class two it all came together and after about two weeks' hard work I could read fluently. This seems to me in hindsight to be the best way of doing things as I should certainly have resented it had I been pushed into it and, as it was, it was painless and easy.

One of the nicest things about the first eight years of my school life was the fact that I had one class teacher who was with me throughout. It certainly made for a more friendly atmosphere as my teacher was very well known to me and if there was a problem I always felt as if there was someone I could talk to.

Main Lesson has been part of my school life from the beginning and it would feel a much stranger place for me without it. Studying in blocks like this allows one to follow threads of a subject right through rather than having to wait for another lesson a week later. It also allows me to continue to study subjects that I'm not taking for GCSE.

In my opinion the Upper School has something incredibly valuable to offer particularly now when academic pressure on young people is enormous. It does not focus solely on exams and one is thus spared the pain of sitting ten exams in a single year.

Crafts tend to form quite a large portion of the timetable (particularly in the middle school and Class nine) and although I do not particularly enjoy all the practical work I appreciate the opportunity to get out of the classroom and away from what can otherwise be a very heavy workload.

Steiner education has had a great impact on my life and has certainly helped to shape who I am and to give me a wider picture of the world I live in. However it is not for everybody and one must be willing to accept things that are unusual and to keep an open mind in order to get the full value from it.

In the future I would certainly consider sending my children to a Steiner school but this would depend very much on which school it was as the Steiner schools are independent and thus some schools are a lot better than others.

Benjamin Murray, aged 16, student, Elmfield School

Iona School
310 Sneinton Dale, Nottingham NG3 7DN
Tel: 0115 958 7392

School established: 1983

Number of pupils on roll: 85

Curriculum: Steiner curriculum

Hereford Waldorf School★
Much Dewchurch, Herefordshire HR2 8DL
Tel: 01981 540221   Fax: 01981 540221
Email: info@herefordwaldorfschool
Website: www.herefordwaldorfschool.org

School established: 1980

Age range of pupils: 3–16

Maximum number of pupils: 250

Number of staff: 15

Curriculum: Steiner curriculum

Michael House Rudolf Steiner School★
The Field, Shipley, Heanor, Derbyshire DE75 7JH
Tel: 01773 718050   Fax: 01773 711784

School established: 1934

Age range of pupils: 3½–16

Maximum number of pupils: 300

Number of staff: 20

Curriculum: Steiner curriculum

Description: Co-educational, non-selective school on a rural site between Nottingham and Derby.

North East

Botton Village School★
Botton Village, Danby, Whitby, North Yorkshire YO21 2NJ
Tel: 01287 661206   Fax: 01287 661207
Email: school.botton@camphill.org.uk

School established: 1960

Age range of pupils: 4–14

Maximum number of pupils: 100

Number of staff: 8 full time, 1 part time

Curriculum: Steiner curriculum

Description: Based in a purpose built village college which also provides for adult education. Approximately half the children come from the adjacent Camphill Village and are children of co-workers at the village, which provides residence and meaningful work for adults with special needs. Situated in the North York Moors National Park near Whitby, York and Middlesborough.

York Steiner School★
Danes Mead, Fulford Cross, York YO10 4PB
Tel: 01904 654983   Fax: 01904 654983

School established: 1980

Age range of pupils: 3½–14

Number of pupils on roll: 192

Number of staff: 27 (including part time)

Curriculum: Steiner curriculum

North West

Lancaster Steiner School
18 Milking Stile Lane, Lancaster LA1 5QB
Tel: 01524 841351

School established: 1995

Age range of pupils: 3–8

Number of pupils on roll: 30

Curriculum: Steiner curriculum

Northern Ireland

Holywood Rudolf Steiner School★
34 Croft Road, Holywood, County Down BT18 0PR
Tel: 02890 428029   Fax: 02890 428029

School established: 1975

Age range of pupils: 4–17

Number of pupils on roll: 135

Curriculum: Steiner curriculum

Republic of Ireland

Raheen Wood School★
Raheen Road, Tuamgraney, Scariff, County Clare
Tel: (00 33) 61 921 494 Fax: (00 33) 61 921 494
Email: cooleen@iol.ie
Website: www.cooleenbridge.home.dhs.org

School established: 1986

Age range of pupils: 3–14

Number of pupils on roll: 100

Curriculum: Steiner curriculum

Scotland

Aberdeen Waldorf School★
Craigton Road, Cults, Aberdeen AB15 9QD
Tel: 01224 868366   Fax: 01224 868316
Email: aws@talk21.com
Website: www.aberdeenwaldorf.co.uk

School established: 1976

Age range of pupils: 3–16

Maximum number of pupils: 250

Number of staff: 8 full time, 12 part time

Curriculum: Steiner curriculum

Description: Situated in 8 acres of grass and woodland on a hillside three miles outside Aberdeen. Extensive views, fresh air and spacious grounds offer unique opportunities for play, physical activity and environmental education.

Edinburgh Rudolf Steiner School*
60 Spylaw Road, Edinburgh EH10 5BR
Tel: 0131 337 3410   Fax: 0131 538 6066
Email: office@SteinerWeb.org.uk
Website: www.SteinerWeb.org.uk

School established: 1939

Age range of pupils: 3½–19

Maximum number of pupils: 350

Number of staff: 60 including administrative, janitorial etc.

Curriculum: Steiner curriculum

Description: Situated in leafy south Edinburgh, 10 minutes by bus from the city centre. Sandstone buildings provide light, airy classrooms for both the Lower and Upper Schools. Our hall gives space for regular pupil performances. The kindergarten, purpose built in its own garden, is designed to stimulate a creative and imaginative start to learning.

A teacher's view
Seen from the outside, teaching in a Steiner school may not look very different from teaching in any other kind of school: children are children and the trials, tribulations, joys and frustrations they bring with them are there too. I look forward to weekends and count down the weeks to the next holiday just as much as any other teacher does, I'm sure. Nevertheless, I am

also sure that I would not have lasted even half the fourteen years I have been teaching, had I not opted to do it in a Steiner school.

Ever since the age of 11, when I went on a school trip to the Loire valley and returned with a set of slides and a mission to explain to all who would sit still long enough the differences between Renaissance and Gothic architecture, I somehow felt I had it in me to be a teacher.

The problem for me was finding the right school – or rather, the right curriculum. To spend my life teaching German verbs day in day out (my qualification was in languages) or training children to jump through arbitrarily arranged hoops, was too narrow and too meaningless to merit consideration, so I never even embarked on a teacher training course – there had to be more in it.

It wasn't until I was 26 and had pretty well given up the idea of teaching, that I found out there was an alternative. Since making the decision to do the Steiner training course I have never looked back.

Picking up a class of 6-year-olds, shaping and building the fabric in the first year, then watching them grow, individually and as a social entity, for the next eight years brings many challenges and many opportunities which would simply never arise if I was only teaching a class for a year or two.

For one thing, it gives me a long-term view of each child's education, knowing that in a year or two's time I will reap the harvest of my efforts in the early years. For another, it means there is never any possibility of getting stuck in a rut. As the children grow, they expect and demand different qualities from me. In the early years they need a clear, calm figure of authority, in whom they can put their total trust. Later they need someone to pit their developing wits against, to argue with, despair at, confront, all in the security of knowing there is a deep bond which will endure any passing crisis. As a teacher, I have to come down off my pedestal, not to be a pal – they have enough of those – but a real person of flesh and blood and feelings, who makes mistakes and learns from them as they do from me.

Perhaps what I enjoy most of all about teaching in a Steiner school is the freedom to explore topics in a multifaceted way, to weave in aspects which I find relevant and interesting, paint a broad canvas which includes many diverse fields of life. Through the medium of the curriculum which Rudolf Steiner set out and which has been developed ever since, I am encouraged to work as an artist, bringing my own skills and interests into the picture too, all in a way which creates an image of the world as a united and meaningful whole and of life as a rich and exciting experience.

This has nothing to do with power or control, but serving a higher aim than just helping the children onto the next rung of the ladder. I really feel that through my teaching, I am giving the children nourishment for life.

Another important difference is the shared responsibility teachers enjoy as colleagues. The absence of a head teacher or any hierarchy means that we all carry the responsibility for our school. We cannot grudgingly accept decisions we don't like for we were all involved in making them, and even if we don't agree with them we know their background. Collegiate working is not always easy, but I believe it is the right way for the future and it gives scope for personal involvement and creative ways of working together.

Lastly, but perhaps most importantly of all, there is the whole philosophical background to Steiner education. Teaching is not just a job, it is a path of self development. In a Steiner school this is openly recognised and time is given within the busy week so that we can help one another become not only better teachers, but wiser, more rounded individuals as well.

Philip Shinton, teacher, Edinburgh Rudolf Steiner School

Glasgow Steiner School
52 Lumsden Street, Yorkhill, Glasgow G3 8RH
Tel: 0141 334 8855

School established: 1988

Age range of pupils: 0–12

Maximum number of pupils: 180

Number of staff: 5 full time, 5 part time

Curriculum: Steiner curriculum

Description: Started as an initiative to bring Steiner education to inner city area with the ideal of not charging set fees. The school currently has four classes between ages 6 and 12.

Moray Steiner School
Drumduan, Clovenside Road, Forres, Moray IV36 2RD
Tel: 01309 676300   Fax: 01309 671092
Email: Welcome@moraysteinerschool.org
Website: www.moraysteinerschool.org

School established: 1985

Age range of pupils: 3½–14

Maximum number of pupils: 112

Number of staff: 14

Curriculum: Steiner curriculum

Description: Set in 7 acres of mature woods and gardens, on a hill overlooking Findhorn Bay and the Moray Firth. A young, dynamic and growing Steiner school. Plans to build an upper school are in progress.

Wales

Nant-y-Cwm Rudolf Steiner School★
Llanycefn, Clynderwen, Pembrokeshire SA66 7QJ
Tel: 01437 563640
Email: info@nant-y-cwm.co.uk
Website: www.nant-y-cym.co.uk

School established: 1979

Age range of pupils: 4–14

Maximum number of pupils: 150

Number of staff: 4 full time, various part time

Curriculum: Steiner curriculum

Description: Set in a rural area of Pembrokeshire amongst the foothills of the Preseli mountains, the kindergarten and main school each have their own grounds on the side of a wooded river valley.

Towy Valley Steiner School
Glasallt Fawr, Llangadog, Carmarthenshire SA19 9AS
Tel: 01550 776214

School established: 1993

Age range of pupils: 3–12

Number of pupils on roll: 15

Curriculum: Steiner curriculum

Special needs schools

South East

The Sheiling School
Horton Road, Ashley, Ringwood, Hampshire BH24 2EB
Tel: 01425 478680 Fax: 01425 478680
Email: sheilingco@aol.com

Age range of pupils: 6–19

Description: This school for children in need of special care provides curative education in a community setting. A warm, secure family base is created in extended households. Sports and other activities take place in 50 acres of fields and woodland.

Philpots Manor School
West Hoathly, East Grinstead, Sussex RH19 4PR
Tel: 01342 810268 Fax: 01342 811363

Age range of pupils: 6–16

Number of pupils on roll: 60

Description: Co-educational boarding school based on the Steiner curriculum for children with emotional and behavioural difficulties who are of average or below average intelligence and who have moderate learning difficulties, mild epilepsy or autistic tendencies. The school is based on a small farm and provides a warm, homely environment.

South West

Cotswold Chine School
Box Village, Near Stroud, Gloucestershire GL6 9AG
Tel: 01453 837550 Fax: 01453 837555

Age range of pupils: 10–16

Number of pupils on roll: 42

Description: Residential school for children with a wide variety of educational, medical, therapeutic, social and behavioural needs. The school takes gifted children as well as the educationally needy. It has a modern approach to the Steiner curriculum with detailed pupil assessments and clear targets. Many pupils sit examinations. The ethos of the school is to provide a high level of care and understanding enabling each pupil to develop and recognise their own special qualities and needs. The school has strong links with the local community and with the Ruskin Mill Further Education Centre.

St Christopher's School
Carisbrooke Lodge, Westbury Park, Bristol BS6 7JE
Tel: 0117 973 3301 Fax: 0117 974 3665

Age range of pupils: 5–19

Number of pupils on roll: 50

Description: A residential school for children with severe to profound learning difficulties, some of whom have mobility problems or behavioural difficulties. The school is divided into a lower and upper school and the curriculum is based on Steiner's principles. In the upper school there is an emphasis on life and work skills. The aim of the school is to help children express their individuality and develop their independence.

The Sheiling School
Thornbury Park, Thornbury, Bristol BS35 1HP
Tel: 01454 412194 Fax: 01454 411860
Email: sheilingschool@thornbury.newnet.co.uk
Website: www.home.newnet.co.uk/thornbury

Age range of pupils: 6–19

Description: This school offers an all-round approach to the needs of the child or adolescent. Six extended households create a social organism which is protective, supportive and challenging.

Midlands

Potterspury Lodge School
Towcester, Northamptonshire NN12 7LL
Tel : 01908 542912 Fax: 01908 543399

Age range of pupils: 8–16

Description: The school is for boys who have a variety of emotional, social and behavioural difficulties including a significant number with Asperger's syndrome. The curriculum includes the National Curriculum and work-based training. Exams can be taken in most subjects. There is particular emphasis on developing creativity. The celebration of seasonal festivals and Sunday services are an integral part of school life.

Sunfield
Clent, Stourbridge, West Midlands DY9 9PB
Tel: 01562 882253 Fax: 01562 883856

Age range of pupils: 6–19

Number of pupils on roll: 85

Description: A residential school based on Steiner's principles for children with severe and complex learning needs including autism, epilepsy, challenging behaviour and language disorder. The emphasis is on meeting children's individual needs. The school is based in 60 acres of parkland.

Scotland

Camphill Rudolf Steiner School
Murtle House, Bieldside, Aberdeen AB15 9EP
Tel: 01224 867935 Fax: 01224 868420
Email: office@crss.org.uk

Cairnlee House, Bieldside, Aberdeen AB15 9BN
Tel: 01224 867251 Fax: 01224 862415
Email: office@cairnlee.clara.net

Age range of pupils: 3–19

Number of pupils on roll: 100

Description: These two schools consist of a nursery and a comprehensive education programme for children with complex educational needs. Pupils live in seventeen extended households and benefit from the school's educational, recreational and therapeutic facilities.

Ochil Tower School
140 High Street, Auchterarder, Perthshire PH3 1AD
Tel: 01764 662416 Fax: 01764 662416
Email: Ochiltowerschool@csi.com

Age range of pupils: 6–17

Number of pupils on roll: 35

Description: The school is situated on a 7 acre estate and takes day and residential pupils.

Teacher training

There are a number of teacher training courses for people wishing to work in Steiner schools. A list of the courses offered around the UK is available from the Steiner Waldorf Schools Fellowship.

For information

Steiner Waldorf Schools Fellowship
Kidbrooke Park
Forest Row
East Sussex
RH18 5JA
Tel: 01342 822115
Fax: 01342 826004
Email: mail@waldorf.compulink.co.uk
Website: www.compulink.co.uk/~waldorf

Further reading

Clouder, C. and Rawson, M. (1998) *Waldorf Education*, Edinburgh: Floris Books.

Edmunds, L. F. (1979) *Rudolf Steiner Education*, London: Rudolf Steiner Press.

Spock, M. (1978) *Teaching as a Lively Art*, London: Anthroposophic Press.

Steiner, R. (1975) *Education of the Child*, London: Rudolf Steiner Press.

Chapter 4

Montessori education

My vision of the future is no longer of people taking exams . . . but of individuals passing from one stage of independence to a higher, by means of their own activity, through their own effort of will, which constitutes the inner evolution of the child.

Maria Montessori, *From Childhood to Adolescence*, 1973

Montessori is a worldwide movement associated particularly with early years education, although increasing numbers of schools are being extended to accept children beyond nursery age. The inspiration behind the movement was Maria Montessori (1870–1952), an Italian doctor, who turned her attention to education. She began by teaching children with special educational needs but her observations led her to believe that the methods she was developing were appropriate for all children. In 1907 she set up her first school, the *Casa dei Bambini* or Children's House, in the San Lorenzo slum district of Rome. Within five years her ideas had spread to the UK. In 1912 the first British Montessori school was opened in Norfolk amidst much discussion in educational circles about the merits of her methods.

Today there are over 700 Montessori registered schools in the UK. The vast majority of these are for early years education. Around eighty take children over the age of six and only ten take secondary aged children. Of those schools which take children beyond the age of six, many combine Montessori's approach with teaching the National Curriculum: only a handful are considered to be pure Montessori schools.

Early years

Maria Montessori believed that children are naturally motivated to learn. They should be allowed to develop and learn at their own, self-directed pace without adult interference. Teachers are called directors or directresses because their role is to guide each child's progress and to provide the appropriate environment to facilitate the learning process. The first Children's House was built with low windows and small furniture to provide a child-orientated setting. It was Montessori's view that children learn through their senses and she designed special objects and materials for use in the classroom. The emphasis is on learning by doing and through real-life, practical activities.

Montessori believed that you cannot be free unless you are independent, so from an early age children are encouraged to do things for themselves, thereby becoming self-reliant. If they don't get it right the first time children are encouraged to try again until, through patience, carefulness and repetition, they succeed. There is no praise or criticism, just the help needed to learn a specific task. The reward is inherent in the accomplishment of the task and it is this that motivates children to achieve.

The learning environment in a Montessori school is generally very ordered, but children have a large degree of freedom to choose their own activities. Such conditions, she believed, developed in children qualities such as self-discipline, concentrated attention and interest and a desire for order. It is a child-centred philosophy in that the needs of the child are the starting point. There is recognition that children are all different and learn in different ways. It is the teacher's responsibility to observe the children closely so that the activities offered are relevant to the stage of development of each child. As far as the content of learning is concerned and the activities which are made available for the children, these are outlined by Montessori.

The materials designed by Montessori include blocks, beads, puzzles and trays of miniature objects. They are designed to teach about shape, size, texture, sound, language and number. She determined the way in which these were to be used with children and even the order in which they were to be introduced. The idea of these materials is that they help children progress from concrete knowledge to the understanding of abstract concepts. They are still used widely in Montessori schools today.

Primary years

There are only a small number of Montessori schools in the UK which teach children right through the primary years, although such schools exist in greater numbers in other parts of the world. The primary classes which do exist in this country build on the philosophy and methods practised in the nursery classes.

Figure 4.1 Using Montessori's materials.
Credit: Maria Montessori School, Exeter and Quay Studios, Exeter

Montessori identified three main characteristics of children as they move into this stage of their development: an interest in the world beyond the classroom and in more abstract concepts, a concern with morality and the development of social awareness. The educational environment and the curriculum are designed around these three areas.

Reading and writing are taught when the child is ready and showing interest, not at a set time. This often takes place around the age of six. National Curriculum subjects are generally covered in Montessori schools but there is an emphasis on drawing out the connections between the different subject areas. Topic work plays a central part.

There is an emphasis on flexibility so that the learning process can be adapted to suit different children's needs. The teacher has a responsibility to create the right emotional climate so that children feel secure but able to take risks. This is seen as an important aspect of learning something new. Children are involved in planning their own work and to an extent they direct their own learning. They are encouraged to evaluate their work, as this is an integral part of becoming independent and taking responsibility for what they do.

There are rules and limits as to what is allowed but the primary aim is to engender self-discipline.

In the early years, education is concerned with the practical aspects of day-to-day living within the security of a home-like environment. At this second stage a concern with more abstract issues begins to emerge and the child asks many questions. This stage is also about venturing into society, so that through their contact with others children develop moral awareness. There is a strong emphasis on peaceful coexistence and showing respect for others. The teacher has to think about how the conscience can be awakened through social interaction and design appropriate activities to support this development. The emphasis here is practical – on doing rather than on talking about it. Children learn together in small groups, establishing a caring and mutually respectful atmosphere.

There is much physical exercise at this stage. Long walks and expeditions are encouraged so that children get used to facing challenges. It is not so much the walk itself which is important but rather what is learned from the experience. Children prepare carefully for going out and think about what they will need. On these outings they learn about weather prediction, orientation and careful observation. Many opportunities for contact with the natural world are provided in order to help children grow into ecologically responsible adults.

During the primary years children continue to take an interest in looking after themselves – their body and their clothes – and this is encouraged as part of the process of developing care and sensitivity.

Adolescence

Many of the principles at play in the early years classroom are equally applicable with much older children. Montessori believed that adolescents need physical exercise, that they need to work with their hands and also to develop their minds.

As far as physical exercise is concerned young people are encouraged to be active rather than being tied to their desks all day. As well as being free to move around in the classroom – to stretch and to exercise as needed – they are encouraged to go for long walks and to work on outdoor projects.

Students use their hands in a variety of ways, in building and gardening, by using a range of tools and equipment and in creative projects such as art, sculpture, stage design and pottery.

Mental development is fostered through dialogue and written work and through reflection. Montessori believed that a major aim for this stage of education is to help young people to think for themselves. Academic education is not seen as an end in itself, nor even as a preparation for a career, but is about enabling young people to make a positive contribution to society through their work. It is at around this time that young people's interest in society is awakened and they begin to develop their own values.

Reflecting these concerns the curriculum for this age group is divided into three parts – self expression, 'psychic' education and preparation for adult life.

Montessori was concerned to develop a sense of responsibility in students, and felt that this was best achieved first by building a respectful community within the school and then by helping older students to establish contact with and serve the community beyond the school. She thought it was important for students to get out of the classroom to meet a wide range of people in the outside world. Equally important is the need to build self-esteem so that students have a sense of their own worth. However this sense of worth must stem from the feeling that the person has something valuable to offer to society – and so the whole process of education is about developing this capacity.

For many years Montessori lectured all over the world and trained her teachers herself. She demanded that teachers who used her methods did so without making any changes. The authoritarian way in which she led the movement has caused subsequent difficulties for practitioners. Some aim to practice her methods in the precise way in which she ordained. Others have a more relaxed approach and place their own interpretation on her ideas. As a result there are several different Montessori organisations in the UK.

Questions often asked about Montessori education

How can Montessori's approach to education be compatible with the National Curriculum?
Some schools feel that they can work with the National Curriculum. The difference is in how it is used, and teachers will apply it in response to individual children's needs. Other schools do not work with it and draw up their own curriculum.

If a child goes to a Montessori nursery until the age of six how easy is it to transfer to a state school?
The key issue concerning how successfully a child will transfer to another school is the extent to which she has developed confidence and self-awareness. These are qualities that a Montessori education seeks to foster and as a rule children who have developed these qualities find it easier to settle into a different school. However it varies from child to child.

What is special about the materials developed by Montessori?
These materials were developed through trial and error and the idea behind them is the *isolation of principle*. What this means is that children can focus on one property of objects without being distracted by others. For example, they can work on shape without being distracted by other features, such as colour or noise. In this way children learn more easily about the properties of objects.

Do Montessori schools charge fees?
Many Montessori schools are part of the government's voucher scheme for nursery education and at these schools fees are not charged for pre-school children. Once children reach school age parents have to pay fees.

List of schools

The following list includes details of schools in England offering Montessori education beyond the early years. A comprehensive list of schools in any particular area is available from the Montessori St Nicholas Centre (contact details are given below).

South East

Holly Park Montessori School
Holly Park Methodist Church Hall, Crouch Hill, London
N4 4BY

Tel: 020 7263 6563 Fax: 020 7263 7022
Email: alake@hpmontessori.fsnet.co.uk

School established: 1986

Age range of pupils: 2–11

Maximum number of pupils: 75

Number of staff: 8 plus outside subject teachers

Curriculum: Montessori curriculum covering English, maths, biology, science, botany, geography, history, art, information and communications technology, religions and festivals of the world, PE, swimming, drama.

Exams offered: No formal exams, only informal assessments/tests.

Description: The school occupies a church hall near Crouch End. It is a small, friendly school where children are able to develop and learn at their own pace as individuals using a wide range of materials. The school aims to help children grow in self-confidence as well as learning to help care for and respect each other and learning to be part of the community.

A teacher's view

I started the Holly Park Montessori School for children aged two to five after having worked at a Montessori school in Battersea. I have always found the Montessori approach to children and learning very thoughtful and caring. Being child-centred it follows the interests of the child rather than the adult's or the school's agenda. As an educational approach it makes sense.

At the school we have always had supportive groups of parents as well as a wonderful staff. There is an atmosphere of warmth, kindness and friendliness in the school, where all are welcome. Right from the beginning there was a core group of parents who were keen to extend the age range beyond five years. Eventually in 1994 we opened our first elementary class for children aged six to nine, one of only a few that have opened in the UK in recent years. This class has been very successful and we hope to extend the age range again as soon as is possible.

I have always believed that a Montessori school should inspire and motivate children to want to learn and that is what we try to do. We offer a balanced curriculum according to the interests of the child. As Montessori teachers we help children to understand the world around them and learn from it by guiding them. They work with beautiful and simple Montessori materials to enable them to grasp concepts without effort. They are helped to become independent by being encouraged to do things for themselves using the materials in the class and are able to choose their own activities. They learn to become part of a community and respect each other and their environment. When I walk into a Montessori class I am always struck by the fact that so many children are all busy doing their own activities and yet there is always a sense of calm, and the children are cooperative and helpful towards each other. The teachers are in the room but are not noticeable, quietly guiding and helping children in their learning, when needed.

Our school is in church premises which were initially very basic, but we have made improvements over the years and now have a garden, children's toilets, a kitchen and extra classrooms upstairs. Unfortunately we have to share part of these premises with other groups. We have been searching for our own permanent premises for many years but the price of property and the difficulty of obtaining it in London makes this an extremely difficult task.

In recent years the school has been adversely affected by directives from the government – the National Curriculum, the numeracy and literacy hours, the Desirable Learning Outcomes and now the Early Years Foundation Stage. The nursery grant, although opening up Montessori schools to more families, means that we are struggling with reams of paperwork which we now have to provide as evidence of learning in order that our families can receive the grant. Of course we also have to be inspected to check that we are following the government's view of good early years education. This depends heavily on the inspector's view of the school. As a well-known Montessori school in the area with a good reputation we have not had any worries so far. We cover all the requirements and have managed to translate the Montessori aims into language Ofsted inspectors understand. But I am not sure how I will feel about this in the future. Our worry is that when state education is becoming so prescriptive will schools like ours have to become the same as more traditional schools in order to survive? I certainly hope not. Will we, as a small organisation, be able to fight our corner and continue to be recognised as offering a separate method of education or will we be ignored? Will the most important thing be a school's position in the league tables? There seems to be less and less diversity in education these days, not more. I hope that the government will realise that more choice is needed, more support for those schools offering something different.

Amanda Lake, founder, Holly Park Montessori School

Meadowbrook Montessori School
Malt Hill, Warfield, Berkshire RG42 6JQ
Tel: 01344 890869   Fax: 01344 890869
Email: mbrookuk@aol.com

School established: 1990

Age range of pupils: 3–12

Maximum number of pupils: 120

Number of staff: 24

Curriculum: Hybrid curriculum encompassing Montessori programme and the National Curriculum.

Description: One of the few schools in England to offer a Montessori education to children up to 11 years. Our small, well-established school is deeply committed to providing children with an educational experience that is truly engaging. Set in 3 hectares of countryside, Meadowbrook works to the ethos of positive discipline and Montessori practice which is based on the belief that children have equal claim to dignity and respect.

Norfolk Lodge Nursery and Preparatory School
Dancers Hill Road, Barnet, Hertfordshire EN5 4RP
Tel: 0208 447 1565   Fax: 0208 440 8575
Email: norfolklodge@hotmail.com
Website: www.timecollege.sagenet.co.uk

School established: 1996

Age range of pupils: 2–11

Maximum number of pupils: 175

Number of staff: 36

Curriculum: 3 to rising 5s – Montessori nursery curriculum; 5 to 11 year olds – National Curriculum plus public speaking and communication skills, a range of sports, music, drama, art and design.

Description: Situated in a large, homely manor house in a rural area with own woodlands and nature trails, a sports pitch, newly built assembly hall. Prep department has no more than twelve children per class, facilitating an individual and personal approach to education and styles of learning. The school is also the home to the TIME college where students train for qualifications as a Montessori teacher.

Primrose Montessori School
Congregational Church, Highbury Quadrant, London N5 2TE
Tel: 0207 359 8985   Fax: 0207 690 4353
Email: andreagrandson@yahoo.com

School established: 1984

Age range of pupils: 2–11

Maximum number of pupils: 130

Number of staff: 12

Curriculum: Guidelines and attainment targets of the Early Learning Goals followed plus the National Curriculum, but uses Montessori philosophy and materials to reach the targets. Dance, drama, French, music, swimming, gymnastics all taught by specialist teachers.

Description: Independent co-educational nursery, infant and primary departments offering day care and education from 8 am to 6 pm Monday to Friday. Teaching takes place in mixed age groups with an individual learning programme for each child. It has developed a successful programme for teaching dyslexic children in mainstream classes. Each child is respected and valued individually thereby increasing confidence and self esteem at all levels. Sixteen pupils per class, pupil/teacher ratio 1:8.

Rainbow Montessori School
13 Woodchurch Road, London NW6 3PL
Tel: 0207 328 8986   Fax: 0207 624 4046
Email: rms@rainbowmontessori.co.uk
Website: www.rainbowmontessori.co.uk

School established: 1982

Age range of pupils: 2½–12

Maximum number of pupils: 100

Number of staff: 12

Curriculum: Pure Montessori approach, covering all subjects and many extras: French, Spanish, guitar, piano, computer, drama, cello, dance.

Description: One of the few Montessori schools that take children through to 12 years. Children learn at their own pace in true Montessori style. A wide variety of subjects offered including sports, many instruments and foreign languages. There are many after-school clubs to pursue any interests.

A parent's view

I first heard about the Montessori method of teaching through my sister in law, who had placed both her sons at Rainbow Montessori School from the age of two-and-a-half. She explained to me that it was an alternative teaching philosophy that focused on the total education of the child and not just the three R's. It was a nursery education designed to give confidence to the child and lay the vital foundations for the child's continued education. After a year at a local Montessori nursery my daughter started at Rainbow Montessori School at the age of four. At this point I still did not understand too much about how it all worked but could see that my daughter was happy and thriving. She would come home from school and proudly show me how she could put on her own coat, tie her own shoes and do many more self-sufficient, confidence-boosting activities. I was impressed with her courtesy and her awareness and respect for others, qualities not usually found in a typical four year old.

Because I was intrigued by my daughter's progress on all levels, I decided to explore further the philosophy and methods of the school. When the proprietor announced the opening of the Rainbow Montessori Teacher Training College I jumped at the chance to join and signed on. The idea of actually becoming a teacher was not my motivation but I felt it might benefit my daughter if I could learn more about the day-to-day teaching methods and discover more about Montessori's philosophy. A year and a half later I graduated and my eyes had been well and truly opened to the superiority of these teaching methods. During this time I also became involved with the *Friends of the Rainbow* charitable arm of the school and eventually became its vice chairman. This group organises all the fund-raising events for the school.

Through these activities my husband and I have made many new friends amongst the teachers and other parents.

Because Maria Montessori believed that all children are born with a desire to learn she developed a method of teaching that was tailor-made to the requirements of their young minds. She made learning fun and because children are encouraged to learn from their own mistakes their lessons are seldom forgotten. I have found her method an invaluable source of inspiration, not only in the classroom but at home and I only wish that I had known of her philosophy before I became a mother.

My only worry has been where to send my daughter after she graduated from Rainbow. This problem has now been resolved as the school is to expand to include children up to the age of 16.

I truly believe that if the Secretary of State for Education made the Montessori method an option for state schools more of our children would graduate as not only literate but also caring, happy and free thinking individuals.

Gil Silvester, parent, Rainbow Montessori School

St Andrew's Montessori Prep
Garston Manor, High Elms Lane, Watford,
Hertfordshire WD25 0JX
Tel: 01923 663875

School established: 1991

Age range of pupils: 0–13

Maximum number of pupils: 200

Number of staff: 16

Curriculum: Montessori-based using National Curriculum and SATs exams

Description: A small friendly school on a 21 acre site including own woodland. Special needs unit. Children staying on for secondary school have their own special programme.

South London Montessori School
Trott Street, Battersea, London SW11 3DS
Tel: 0207 738 9546   Fax: 0207 622 2904

School established: 1990

Age range of pupils: 2½–12

Maximum number of pupils: 42

Number of staff: 8

Curriculum: Pure Montessori curriculum

Description: Montessori education up to the age of 12. Aims to provide an environment that helps to develop in each child self-confidence and an ability to learn independently.

Willow Tree Montessori School
Charlwood House, Charlwood Road, Lowfield Heath, Crawley
RH11 0QA
Tel: 01293 565544   Fax: 01293 611705

School established: 1995

Age range of pupils: 6 months–11

Maximum number of pupils: 75

Number of staff: 16

Curriculum: National Curriculum and Montessori philosophy

Description: Founded as a Montessori Kindergarten over ten years ago. School venues are in Crawley and Horley. Expanded into a primary school in 1995, in response to demands from parents.

South West

Lanherne Nursery and Junior School
18 Longlands, Dawlish, Devon
Tel: 01626 863091
Email: Lanherneschool@aol.com

School established: 1980

Age range of pupils: 6 months–11

Maximum number of pupils: 70

Number of staff: 10

Curriculum: Montessori based curriculum

Description: Independent, family atmosphere. Small group sizes to ensure individual attention. Large, well-equipped gardens offering space to develop outside interests.

East Anglia

Hadleigh Montessori School
Ipswich Road, Hadleigh, Suffolk IP7 6BG
Tel: 01473 828682
Email: cherylprentice@btinternet.com
Website: Montessori-suffolk.sch.uk

School established: 1993

Age range of pupils: 0–13

Maximum number of pupils: School 60, Nursery 54

Number of staff: School 4, Nursery 9

Curriculum: Full Montessori curriculum

Description: Small school with specialist teachers on staff for specific learning difficulties (e.g. dyslexia). It trains its own Montessori assistants to ensure consistency of provision throughout the school. Classes are multi-age, in three groups so that the older children lead by example and help the younger ones.

Midlands

Terrace Montessori School
23 Milverton Terrace, Leamington Spa, Warwickshire CV32 5BE
Tel: 01926 312523   Fax: 01926 312523
Email: TerraceUK@aol.com

School established: 1999

Age range of pupils: 3–16

Maximum number of pupils: 50

Number of staff: 5

Curriculum: According to the needs of the child with awareness of the contents and structure of the National Curriculum

Description: Provides a child-centred, holistic education with a multi-sensory approach. The Montessori philosophy is followed throughout the school with one of the central principles being 'freedom with discipline'. Teachers, parents and pupils work closely together in this community school to develop the child's full potential. Local facilities are used whenever possible.

A teacher's view
As a full-time directress at the Terrace School, I am responsible for a group of lively, spontaneous and enthusiastic children aged between 2 years 9 months and 6 years old. We work and play alongside the other two teachers and their groups in one large hall – a true learning community. The atmosphere is serene and calm as the children throw themselves into their learning with varying amounts of direction. The mix of ages brings a special magic and there is nothing so wonderful as seeing a 12 year old, gawky boy gently reading a story to the little 3 year old on his knee. I find the school an inspiring place to grow and am thankful to be a part of it.

Celia Lowe, Directress, The Terrace School

North East

Glen House Montessori School
Cragg Vale, Hebden Bridge, West Yorkshire HX7 5SQ
Tel: 01422 884682
Email: margret@glenhouseschool.freeserve.co.uk
Website: www.glenhouseschool.freeserve.co.uk

School established: 1986

Age range of pupils: 2½–15

Maximum number of pupils: 35

Number of staff: 6

Curriculum: Montessori curriculum (individual study) in mornings. Afternoons include group activities such as yoga and meditation, group discussion, class meeting, science (including gardening), cultural studies, art, music, drama, cooking.

Description: Situated in the Calder Valley, in a large country house in its own grounds with a large sheltered grass playground and other play areas. The school has its own organic garden, where children are actively involved in all stages of land preparation and vegetable growing. The school opens four days per week and children can attend on a full- or part-time basis.

A student's view
I really like my school for a lot of reasons. For a start there are no school uniforms and yucky school dinners, we all bring our own lunch but there are restrictions in one way like no sweets or plain chocolate. There is also a long playtime so I can make friends better and play longer, which is good because some of us like me live a long way away from the school and most of my friends. I find it easier to learn things because of the apparatus and materials and it is good that you do not have to learn the same as everyone else. You can go ahead or stay behind until you understand it. It is more peaceful because there are less people in one room than in a state school, like in my room there are about 13 children ranging from 7 to 12. We all do different things which we can choose ourselves, but sometimes we do things together. These are mostly all the reasons I like this school. THIS SCHOOL IS GREAT!!!

Michaela Queitsch, aged 11, Glen House Montessori School

Hearter Montessori
West Cliffe School, 206 Skipton Road, Keighley, West Yorkshire
BD21 2TA
Tel: 01535 609797
Email: heartermontessori@hotmail.com

School established: 1998

Age range of pupils: 0–13

Maximum number of pupils: 45

Number of staff: 6

Curriculum: Montessori curriculum is followed incorporating the best practice from maintained/traditional schools

Other sources of funding: Nursery education grant for 3–4 year olds

Description: The school offers a balanced range of experiences in a caring environment. Children can progress at their own pace, without pressure, encouraged to develop in whatever direction they choose. It aims to cultivate the child's own natural desire to learn. Children are taught in small classes where they are well known by their teachers.

Wharfedale Montessori School and College
Strid Cottage, Bolton Abbey, Skipton, North Yorkshire, BD23 6AN
Tel: 01756 710452   Fax: 01756 710452
Email: jane.lord@virgin.net

School established: 1990

Age range of pupils: 2–12

Maximum number of pupils: 50

Number of staff: 8 plus 3 ancillary

Curriculum: We follow the Montessori approach and philosophy fully and incorporate computers and technology as appropriate

Description: True Montessori establishment in an idyllic location on an SSSI nature reserve. Operates as one of Montessori Centre International's part-time regional colleges. Offers five-day residential courses all year round for those wishing to find out about Montessori or take refresher courses.

For information

Montessori Centre International
18 Balderton Street
London W1K 6TG
Tel: 0207 493 0165
Fax: 0207 629 7808
Email: mci@montessori.ac.uk

Website: www.montessori.ac.uk
Provides teacher training in Montessori's methods. Publishes a quarterly magazine. The college shop sells Montessori learning materials and books.

Montessori Education (UK) Ltd
21 Vineyard Hill
London SW19 7LJ
Tel: 0207 433 1548
Fax: 0208 944 6920
Training organisation for teachers. Also provides information service on schools and sets standards for school evaluation.

The Montessori Society AMI (UK)
26 Lyndhurst Gardens
London NW3 5NW
Tel: 0207 435 7874
Provides information about Montessori principles, organises events and sells publications and other materials. Produces a list of AMI (Association Montessori Internationale) run Montessori schools in the UK.

Montessori St Nicholas Centre
23–24 Princes Gate
London SW7 1PT
Tel: 0207 584 9987
Comprehensive list of Montessori schools in the UK available. Also funds research into the value and effectiveness of Montessori education.

Further reading

Kramer, R. (1976) *Maria Montessori, A Biography*, London: Montessori International Publishing.
Lilliard, P. (1972) *Montessori, A Modern Approach*, New York: Schocken Books.
Montessori, M. (1918) *The Advanced Montessori Method*, London: Heinemann.
Montessori, M. (1973) *From Childhood to Adolescence*, New York: Schocken Books.

Chapter 5

Democratic schools

> The only form of society which facilitates the continued evolution
> of the human species is a democratic form of society, and further-
> more, the development of such a democratic society is dependent
> to a large degree on the democratisation of schools and schooling.
>
> John Dewey

You can take a horse to water but you cannot make it drink. The same
can be said of education: you cannot force a child to learn. Children
learn only if they want to, if they are interested and if the conditions
are right: real learning, that is, not the ability to parrot facts or to
reproduce undigested information. So how do you create a school
which children want to go to and where they want to learn? The best
way, arguably, is to ask the children themselves and involve them in the
design and organisation of the school.

This is the basis of democratic schools – that children have a say in
what they learn, when and how they learn it and in how their school
is run. Given the current interest in the notion of teaching children
about citizenship, democratic schools take this idea to its natural
conclusion. They allow children to learn how to make decisions, to take
responsibility for those decisions and to learn from the consequences
of those decisions through experience. Mistakes and bad decisions will
inevitably be made on occasions, but people learn from their mistakes
and bad decisions can always be reversed.

Whilst lessons about the meaning of democracy and the meaning of
citizenship can be taught in a classroom, it takes practice to become a
good citizen and an active participant in society. Democratic schools
are founded on the idea that these skills should be acquired at school
as part of everyday life. Young people who are used to functioning in a

democratic way are more likely to function effectively in a democratic society after leaving school. At a time when there is considerable concern about the lack of political interest and involvement amongst young people this is an important point.

There is a loose alliance of democratic schools across the world in countries as diverse as New Zealand, Japan, Thailand, India, Israel, Ecuador and America, but they are thinly spread. These schools are all very different, depending to a large extent on the people who have set them up and the local situation. In the UK there are currently only two truly democratic schools – Summerhill and Sands – both of which are independent and fee-paying, although a number of others incorporate some democratic principles.

Summerhill

Summerhill is the parent of the whole democratic school movement. It was started by A. S. Neill in the early 1920s and Neill's philosophy has influenced educators the world over ever since. It is perhaps the most famous of all alternative schools. Neill's idea in creating Summerhill was to 'make the school fit the child – instead of making the child fit the school'.

Summerhill is a boarding school where children go to lessons as and when they please. Rules are made by the whole school at a weekly general school meeting. The idea behind the school is that children are free to be themselves. Neill believed that children are innately good and, left to make their own decisions in an atmosphere free of fear, will develop in their own, individual way. When new students join the school they may not go to a lesson for weeks, months or in some cases years but this does not mean they are not learning. There are important lessons to learn beyond those in the classroom and Neill was sure that Summerhill children developed their personality, self-confidence and originality to a much greater extent than their contemporaries in conventional schools. He did not even feel that the teaching was particularly important because if children wanted to learn something, they would learn it regardless. Summerhill children take exams but do so out of choice rather than compunction and are thus likely to be better motivated. According to Neill, if a child is inclined to become an academic she will become an academic in spite of, not because of, her education.

There is a timetable of lessons every morning and children choose what they go to. They are divided into classes roughly according to age.

Figure 5.1 Summerhill School takes a vote.

Credit: Summerhill School

If a child starts to go to a particular course and then after a while only attends spasmodically she may be chastised by the other children for holding them back. Afternoons are free: children can do as they please. For some this means playing in the grounds with friends, others get involved with specific projects in arts or crafts or in the workshop. In the early evening there are further activities which the children can choose from.

The school, now owned by Neill's daughter Zoe Readhead, has not had a completely trouble-free history and has recently been under threat of closure from the Department for Education and Skills (DfES). Repeated visits from inspectors resulted in allegations that health and safety requirements were not being met, but the real battle was over the curriculum and the freedom of the children to attend lessons as and when they pleased. The school was required by Ofsted to make lessons compulsory, which they refused to do as this freedom is the key feature of the school's philosophy. An historic High Court decision in 1999 saved the school but the battle was long and hard fought. There has been an agreement to leave the school alone for the time being, but whether inspectors are encouraged to pitch in again in the future for another round remains to be seen.

This was perhaps the first time that any government has become so embroiled in the affairs of an independent school. Why they were so determined to close down a school which is chosen and paid for entirely by the parents of children who attend, the majority of whom are from overseas (mainly Japan and America) is a moot point. The school has certainly not been helped by negative media coverage either. Presumably people who do not understand what the school is trying to do feel threatened by its difference and are thus prepared to put considerable effort into seeing it destroyed. It is a radical school – in many ways it is at one end of the educational spectrum – but it serves a valuable purpose as such and has been a source of inspiration to many. Research has been done, much has been written about it over the years and there are some very successful alumni in a wide range of careers. In Neill's terms, of course, that is not the point. In his view it is more important that people are happy in their chosen work.

The school has had some remarkable successes with a number of children who were completely turned off education and would have 'failed' miserably anywhere else. Different children thrive in different educational environments and the children who attend Summerhill say that it is perfect for them.

A teacher's view

I started teaching at Summerhill nearly four years ago. I came to the school as an experienced teacher having taught at private schools in the UK and most recently in a State High School in America. My wife had been a student at Summerhill in the 1960s and had always wanted to work there, so when the opportunity arose for us both to get jobs there at the same time, as well as for our children to become students, we jumped at it, right across the Atlantic from California.

Knowing something about the school helped with the transition, but knowing the theory and living it are two different things altogether. For example, Summerhill is a democratic community where students and staff live on an equal footing. Just because you are an adult does not grant you any special status at Summerhill. Despite my intellectual acceptance of this idea, like many adults preceding me here, this issue proved one of the first of my many personal growth experiences. It came about when I was in the queue for lunch, which winds around the wall by the kitchen hatch. While I was waiting, I stepped out of the queue to look at a notice across the waiting area. On returning to my place, I was told by a number of students that I was now at the back of the queue. My first telltale reaction was indignation, followed by adult blustering, all to no avail, as I was firmly told to go to the back of the queue, which I did. I realised that as an adult I could not unconsciously be an authority over kids here, as perhaps I might have been able to do in a regular school, where I was an 'important' teacher. How refreshing!

Another great realisation I had was when covering for one of the house parents at bedtime. I hardly had to do anything. The young kids were ushered in by the big kids in their democratically elected role as bedtime officers or 'beddies'. They made sure the younger ones got changed, cleaned their teeth, got into bed on time, and checked to make sure they stayed there, fining them for any transgressions of the community bedtime laws. My role seemed to consist primarily of unlocking the cupboard and giving out biscuits. Instead of the usual adult authoritarian role I unconsciously expected, the older students were taking on this important job, and doing it brilliantly. It was great to have the freedom of not being in that role all the time.

The adults in the Summerhill community have to learn and grow too, to survive! That is what makes working here interesting, intense and rewarding. Lessons are completely optional, but I found many students came to lessons. Teaching was relatively easy in the small classes, although there were lots of them – nearly thirty-five for me as maths teacher. The students concentrated well and wanted to learn. Of course, there were times when they did not come, and as all teachers here come to discover, I too had to go through the self-questioning of whether my empty classroom was because of something I had done. I learned more about the factors affecting lesson attendance later, when I asked one of the students about this. He told me the lessons were fine, it was just that he had lots of other things to do, and in fact really wanted to socialise right now. That opened my eyes, making me see how one aspect of teaching is easy for a teacher in a regular school, where you have a captive audience. And how artificial too – learning is a natural process, and works best when there is an interest and self generated motivation. The captive audience has a number of choices – to either make the best of it, suffer in silence, rebel or of course enjoy every minute of it because it is just the thing they want to do. If my own schooling is anything to go by, I spent most of my time in the first two modes and never in the last.

Another big impression came from the twice-weekly school meetings. They are superb examples of the student's growth, responsibility and maturity. Chaired by an older student, these meetings offer the opportunity for anyone to change the community rules, the 'laws', and the chance to 'bring someone up' if your personal rights have been infringed in any way. Even the youngest children bring up cases or have a big kid or houseparent bring it up for them. The kids being brought up can be fined – tea biscuits fine or back of the lunch queue were popular choices and acted as very effective feedback from the community. I saw that people were learning to be responsible for themselves and their actions, and how to get on with others. This confirmed another early impression – the students were friendly, tolerant and patient. They learned this, like we all have to, through their own experience, and through being given the chance to learn it. It made total sense, and was so obviously important – this was real education.

There are lots of chances for the students to take more responsibility in the community when they are ready. One of the great Summerhill innovations is the use of older students as Ombudsmen to resolve arguments and disputes. The students understand the value of this and use Ombudsmen a lot. The Ombudsmen work very hard, but learn a tremendous amount too. Obviously Summerhill is not a perfect utopian existence, but it is a very practical place, which has developed structures and ways of doing things that allow the process of living, especially emotional living, to have the active arena it needs. The use of Ombudsmen is one such process.

The community is really well racially integrated. Students from all over the world live here. I found I quickly accepted people for who they were, irrespective of where they were born. I did not realise this for some time. One day I walked to the local supermarket with a group of Taiwanese students, happily talking. When I walked into the supermarket I was suddenly struck by the attention focused on them: they were different! I had not thought of them in that way at all.

Ian Warder, teacher, Summerhill

Sands

Sands School in Devon, the second democratic school in the UK, has quite a different feel. It was set up in 1987 after Dartington Hall School, one of the great progressive schools of the twentieth century, closed down. Sands was designed by students and staff who together set out to create their ideal school. Teachers and students have an equal voice in all decisions concerning the running of the school although some areas, for example finance, are delegated. Because there are more students than staff this sometimes results in staff being overruled at the weekly school meeting. It is at this meeting that all important decisions concerning the school are made. Teachers are appointed by the meeting, new students are accepted or rejected, the timetable is agreed and smaller matters of individual concern are also discussed.

The school is based on the idea that children get most out of their education if they themselves make choices about what they are going to study. A broad curriculum is offered and the students, in consultation with parents and teachers, choose which courses they will take each year. Once they have signed up to a course this signals their commitment to attend over the year. Whilst they are free not to attend lessons if they so please – and many take up this freedom on different occasions – on the whole, students attend the courses they have chosen. If a student seems to be absenting herself on a regular basis the teacher will make it his business to seek her out to find out why. This system puts considerable pressure on teachers to be good and to make their lessons interesting. If they are not most children will vote with their feet. They see no reason why they should be subjected to boring lessons which generally have the effect of turning them off a subject.

David Gribble, one of the founders of Sands, says that the school operates on the premise that 'children are trusted, respected and cared for because that is the treatment they deserve'. They certainly take their responsibility seriously and use it wisely. That everyone in the school community is on equal terms breeds an openness and honesty in relationships which make it a very relaxed and easy environment to be in.

Sands started with fourteen children and now has over sixty. The school is going from strength to strength and believes that there is much that conventional schools can learn from its democratic practices.

A student's view

I have been to four schools in my life with varying success. I've never really been understood. They told me I was emotionally and behaviourally disturbed and I wasn't disciplined. Only my mum saw me and tried to show who I really was. Sands was the only school that seemed to listen.

I live alone with my mum and I did my previous schooling in Oxford. I used to go to a school that was perhaps the epitome of brutal. There was hate, fear, cold, intimidation, cruelty and discrimination in the school. I began to harden; to lose my gentle, sensitive, caring side. I was turned to stone on the inside, each day at the place another weathering of my soul, breaking it away into sand. I can say nothing less than that Sands saved me. I felt as though I was drowning and found a piece of wood to float on. My way of describing Sands is that it is like going to a friend's house but with all the resources and motivation to learn anything in just the way you need.

I have been to one other school in which I made a genuine, warm relationship with someone else there; it was a teacher. At Sands, everybody is either a friend, brother, sister, mum, dad or just neutral with me. Look at me! I would have fainted if I saw myself now, back then. I feel mature, like I have learned things that you don't find in the little quiz sheets the 'robot teachers' would hand out to everybody in the class, regardless of whether you'd already completed it thrice. I have been finding bits of my personality jigsaw, piecing myself together, making myself whole. I feel no peer pressure or intimidation at Sands. I am as natural as can be, just as I would act at home, comfortable, calm, open, relaxed. I love it. I dreamed about a system like this. The environment you are in changes your attitude, directly affecting your educational skills. I will tell you a bit about how effective the approach at Sands is.

There is a lot of scepticism about how laid back Sands is. It is true because it is the responsibility of the student to remember lessons and go to them. If you don't feel in the mood to go to lessons you needn't go, but it does help you to discipline yourself if you are the person saying when to go to lessons and not someone else mothering you. Also if you are forced to participate in a lesson when your mind is on something else and you feel restless and non-committal you aren't going to be constructive in that lesson. You might actually disturb another who is and be generally destructive during the period.

Sands has been a roller coaster of experiences for me and gave me new visions from which I have learned much. This is my story of Sands.

Luke Flegg, ex-student, Sands

Questions often asked about democratic schools

Will the child in later life resent not having being forced to learn maths or French for example?

If children want to learn something they will learn it if the opportunities to learn are provided. If they are interested and motivated they will learn much more quickly. At democratic schools children may not study so many different subjects but those that they do take are gone into in greater depth as children engage more fully with the subject matter. Most children do take the core subjects, giving them a basic grounding which they can build on if they so wish.

What happens if a child refuses to go to lessons for an extended period of time?

Eventually they get bored. It may take a long time for them to decide to go to lessons if they are very disaffected, but sooner or later they will start to go. And if they choose lessons that they want to go to it is more likely that they will be motivated to study.

What if children pass a rule that allows smoking/alcohol/ drugs/sex?
First, children are only allowed to do things that are legal. Second, although teachers only have one vote, the same as everyone else and can easily be outvoted, they do have a say in discussions and their views are often listened to. Third, if a rule is made and it turns out to be antisocial, it is highly likely that it will be overturned very quickly.

List of schools

South West

Sands School
48 East Street, Ashburton, Devon TQ13 7AX
Tel: 01364 653666   Fax: 01364 653666
Email: Enquiry@sandsschool.demon.co.uk
Website: www.sandsschool.demon.co.uk

School established: 1987

Age range of pupils: 10–16

Maximum number of pupils: 65

Number of staff: 9

Curriculum: A range of subjects offered and a teaching style that focuses on the needs of the individual

Description: Sands School began as a result of students and staff collaborating to design an ideal place of learning which values the need for academic and technical qualifications and developing students' emotional and social skills, which are felt to be as important as any qualifications achieved during their school career.

The core philosophy of the school is based on the common-sense view that in order to get the most out of an education, you have to make real choices about what you want to do.

East Anglia

Summerhill
Westward Ho! Leiston, Suffolk IP16 4HY
Tel: 01728 830540   Fax: 01728 830540
Email: office@summerhillschool.co.uk
Website: www.s-hill.demon.co.uk

School established: 1921

Age range of pupils: 4–17

Maximum number of pupils: 75

Number of staff: 12

Curriculum: Usual school subjects offered to GCSE but main concern is with personal development through democracy and freedom

Description: The oldest children's democracy in the world, founded by the late A. S. Neill. Works on a principal of freedom for the individual through equality and self-government in a democratic community.

Further reading

Gribble, D. (1998) *Real Education, Varieties of Freedom*, Bristol: Libertarian Education.
Harber, C. (1996) *Small Schools and Democratic Practice*, Nottingham: Educational Heretics Press.
Neill, A. S. (1937) *That Dreadful School*, London: Jenkins.
Neill, A. S. (1962) *Summerhill*, London: Pelican.

Chapter 6

Other philosophies, other schools

> It is because children are not alike, their parents are not alike, their interests are unlike and their needs are unlike that they need different kinds of schools.
>
> Lord Young of Dartington, 'Choice in education',
> *Resurgence*, 1988

A number of different educational philosophers, promoting a child-centred approach to learning, continue to influence educators around the world. This chapter offers a sample, chosen because of the extent of their influence in other countries today.

John Dewey was an American philosopher who wrote widely about education. Whilst there are few schools devoted entirely to putting his ideas into practice, he is a key figure in educational philosophy and his ideas continue to influence educators the world over. The philosophy of Grundtvig has strongly influenced educational practice throughout Denmark, nowhere more so than in the small independent schools of the Free School Movement. Jenaplan schools offer a well-established alternative in Holland where they are fully funded by the state. Freinet's work is well known in his native France but his sphere of influence is much wider and his ideas are put into practice by teachers in state and alternative schools throughout Europe, though he is little known in the UK. The early years nurseries and infant schools of Reggio Emilia in northern Italy are fully state funded. They have been so successful that educationalists from all over the world have visited in great numbers and are working to apply the ideas in their home countries.

John Dewey

John Dewey (1859–1952) was an American philosopher and educator whose ideas have had a huge influence on education in America and further afield. Whilst there is currently only one school in existence named after him, a number of philosophies and approaches have built on work that he did. Dewey was professor of philosophy and psychology at the University of Chicago, during which time he set up the Laboratory School for children connected with the University. This school (which only lasted for seven years) was a test bed for his ideas.

Dewey believed that the purpose of education was to encourage reflective, creative and responsible behaviour and to promote personal growth and health. His view was that education is based on experience and it was therefore the role of the teacher to create the kinds of experiences and the kind of environment which would help the child to develop. The teacher needed to know each child well so as to be able to provide an appropriate programme. What children learned had to have relevance for their life beyond school.

A major purpose of education was, he considered, to encourage the individual to participate in society. For Dewey it was a social process and the school as an organisation had to find the balance between the needs of the individual and of the wider group; between freedom and responsibility. The emphasis was on creating a community within which the child could be helped towards moral responsibility so that pupils would become involved in creating a better world. Education was thus about cultural renewal as well as cultural transmission.

Such a process could best take place within an organisation which was democratic and in which there was a sense of freedom. The teacher, as a member of this community, was seen as a guide, helping the child to achieve certain purposes rather than as an authoritarian figure whose role was to instruct. This new view of the role of the teacher alongside the involvement of children in planning their own studies represented a major shift and has had far-reaching ramifications.

Dewey questioned the value of a subject-based approach to education, believing that the child's life and interests should be at the centre of the curriculum. He saw life and therefore education as consisting of communication, inquiry, construction and artistic expression. Learning was seen as an active process involving much experiment and practical work, especially for younger children. Traditional subjects had their place, but within the context of a wider purpose and only where the child's interest was engaged and where such study would lead to positive growth. Much emphasis was placed on the scientific method of learning which involved setting up and testing hypotheses. This dual approach of reflective thought and action combined to make education into a means of bringing about social change.

Grundtvig and the Danish Free Schools

Around 12 per cent of children in Denmark attend independent, privately run but publicly funded *friskoler* or free schools. There are 430 such schools and over 200 of them belong to the Danish Free Schools Association, which is inspired by Grundtvig.

N. F. S. Grundtvig (1783–1872) is in many senses the father of modern Denmark. As well as being an educational reformer he was a clergyman and politician and his ideas about life and freedom permeate Danish society. His view that spiritual development is the most important task of education, over and above the development of formal competencies, has been of central importance in Denmark and has influenced state schools as well as those of the Free Schools Association.

The free schools grew out of the ideal that children are first and foremost the responsibility of their parents and that parents should have the right to choose how they are educated. Funding is available for those wishing to establish their own school. Grundtvig believed that democracy entailed rights for minorities and that economic support should be given to sustain these rights. Funding is therefore also available to minority groups wishing to set up schools.

There are five principles of freedom which underpin free schools – ideological freedom which allows the school to be based on a political, religious or pedagogical ideology, pedagogical freedom to decide on the curricular content and methods, economic freedom to decide how to use the budget, particularly in respect of fees and salaries, freedom of employment enabling schools to decide who can teach there and finally the freedom to decide which students to accept.

The Grundtvigian free schools all subscribe to Grundtvig's philosophy in that they are characterised by democratic attitudes and organisation. They emphasise teaching through the living word using narrative and song, as he believed that it is through 'living interaction' that a connection is made between the past and the present, the body and the spirit and between teachers and students. Learning is thus an active and participatory pursuit. Over and above these basic principles each school operates differently, reflecting the priorities of the parents and the local community. Parents are closely involved in decision-making and in running the school. Grundtvig's philosophy is founded on Christianity and most of the free schools in this tradition are permeated by Christian values. They all put the child first, however, over and above teaching methods or religious dogma.

The state finances 75 per cent of the costs of free schools in Denmark. If a group of parents wishes to set one up, as long as there are twelve children in the first year rising to a minimum of twenty-eight in the third year, they are entitled to this funding. The remaining 25 per cent is raised from fees but these are kept as low as possible so that all parents can have the possibility of sending their child to such a school.

Jenaplan

The Jenaplan approach to education was developed by Peter Petersen (1884–1952) at an experimental school at the University of Jena in Germany. This approach has taken root not in Germany but in Holland, where the first Jenaplan School opened in 1960. Since then many more have been established and there are now over 200 such schools, the majority of which are publicly funded. Most are primary schools taking children aged 4–12 but there are also a small number of secondary schools for children up to the age of fifteen. Each Jenaplan school has its own characteristics depending on local circumstances, but they all subscribe to the same philosophy.

The philosophy is underpinned by twenty basic principles, five of which are about the person, five about society and ten about schools. The main idea is that each person is a unique individual who should be treated with dignity. The educational process is about helping the child develop a sense of identity. People must work together in such a way that there is room for others to develop their own identity and acknowledges the differences between people. There must be a commit-ment to dealing with such differences in fair and peaceful ways. People must show respect and care for each other and for the earth.

The school is seen as an autonomous and cooperative organisation and there is an emphasis on living and working together collaboratively. Each class contains mixed age groups. The kindergarten takes children aged 4–6 and there are separate classes for children aged 6–9 and 9–12. Secondary schools take children aged 12–15. Such mixed aged groupings are considered essential in helping children develop social skills by learning to be part of a group. The school endeavours to make each group as diverse as possible in terms of interests, ability and social background.

There is an integrated curriculum, at the centre of which is the concept of world orientation whereby children learn about eight different 'fields of experience' – all year round, our environment, making and using, technology, communication, living together, my body and my own life. There is an emphasis on using children's inner experiences alongside cultural sources as a means of helping the child to develop. Additional mixed age interest classes are offered for subjects such as music, dance, art, physics, chemistry, woodwork and photography. Teaching and learning take place through dialogue, play, work and celebration. Children are given the opportunity to make choices about what to learn and much discussion is carried out in a circle, where planning, evaluating, making arrangements and talking about behaviour are discussed democratically.

In the kindergarten the focus is very much on developing social skills through play, drama and construction as well as home activities. Formal learning does not start until the age of six. Literacy is the focus of the intermediate class but children do not start learning to read until they are considered to be ready. The process of learning to read is tied in very closely with topic work. Because of the mixed age classes there is little whole class teaching; instead children are grouped together according to their level of achievement.

There are four teacher training colleges which specialise in Jenaplan in Holland.

Freinet

Célestin Freinet was born in France in 1896 and died in 1966. After serving in the First World War he started his career in teaching in 1921. Freinet was a communist and his aim, from the outset, was to improve the social conditions for children from labouring families. He believed that this could be achieved through education and was extremely critical of the public education system. His ideas about education were underpinned by his concept of productive work. Freinet saw work as the basis of human activity and believed that personal development followed from working productively. After several years of teaching he introduced the Learning Printing Technique whereby students wrote down their experiences and these were reproduced using a printing press. The texts were then discussed and edited by the whole class and collected together in a class journal and a school newspaper.

Students were encouraged to go out into the locality to study both the natural environment and their local community as Freinet believed in an active approach to learning which bore relation to children's lives outside school. The results of these investigations were also compiled into journals. It was a child–centred approach to learning in which children constructed their own plan of work which they discussed and evaluated with their teacher. There was an emphasis on working cooperatively and the class met as a group on a regular basis to coordinate their activities and to address any problems that had arisen.

Freinet made contact with other teachers who were using innovative teaching methods similar to his own and arranged that the newspapers and journals produced by the students were exchanged with other schools. Over time these writings spread throughout the world. Some teachers extended his methods by using sound recordings and film with their students.

In 1928 French teachers working with these techniques founded the Public Educators' Cooperative, which later evolved into the Freinet Movement. This group produced a magazine called *The Proletarian Educator* and also their own materials for teachers. Members shared the belief that traditional textbooks were out of date and largely irrelevant. Amongst their publications were the *Self-Correcting Files* which enabled students to work on improving their skills in particular areas such as maths, grammar and spelling at their own pace.

Freinet was seen as a threat by the local authority which tried to move him to another area. They failed in this, but he eventually left the public school system. In 1935 he set up an independent school at which he further developed his methods. This school closed temporarily when Freinet was sent to an internment camp because of his political activities, but it reopened in 1945. At this point the whole Freinet Movement underwent a revival and the Institut Coopératif de l'Ecole Moderne was founded to take the ideas forward.

Although the work of Célestin Freinet is relatively unknown in the UK there are educators across the rest of Europe, from early years through to university education, who continue to be influenced by his ideas.

Reggio Emilia

Reggio Emilia in northern Italy is home to an inspirational model of early years education which, over the past twenty years, has spread throughout the world. The work is based on the ideas of Piaget,

Vygotsky and Dewey. These ideas have been developed and applied by Loris Malaguzzi whose image of the child was 'rich in potential, strong, powerful, competent and, most of all, connected to adults and other children'. Children are seen as having rights as well as needs.

Around one third of all children in the city up to the age of six are educated at one of a network of over thirty schools which have been created by Malaguzzi and his contemporaries. The schools are run democratically by parents, teachers and the local community. The emphasis is on following the children's interests and allowing them to determine what is learned. Discussion is encouraged to enable learning and understanding to take place through talking and listening. These schools aim to help children make meaning out of their own experiences and facilitate the kinds of interaction, between children and with adults, which lead to learning. At the heart of this programme is 'a vision of children who can think and act for themselves'.

The teacher is seen as a learner or researcher, always experimenting with new ideas. Nothing is cast in stone; rather the teacher tries different things to find out what works in each particular situation.

The emphasis is on providing a loving and caring environment so that children feel safe and part of a large family. Babies and very young children are provided with a wide range of sensory experiences. Art and creativity play a central part and each school has its own art teacher and a well-stocked art room containing all sorts of materials, many of them recycled. The artwork which is produced is of an exceptionally high quality.

One of the innovative aspects of these schools is the way in which they involve parents in the education of their children. Parents are drawn in at all levels – in running the schools, in discussions about the educational work and in playing and learning with their children. In this way the experience becomes embedded in the way that parents bring up their children and this is the key to the success of this approach

A wealth of research in recent years has indicated the importance of early years education in reducing disaffection and delinquency later on. This model has been instrumental in community regeneration.

There are no schools in the UK which are based directly on any of the educational ideas and approaches outlined above, although some schools have been influenced by one or other of them. There are however a number of different schools which have been inspired by philosophies not covered in this book, and these are listed below. All of these schools are independent and charge fees.

List of schools

South East

Brockwood Park School
Bramdean, Nr Alresford, Hampshire SO24 0LQ
Tel: 01962 771744   Fax: 01962 771875
Email: admin@brockwood.org.uk
Website: www.brockwood.org.uk

School established: 1969

Age range of pupils: 15–19

Maximum number of pupils: 60

Number of staff: 27

Curriculum: Offers a personalised programme of studies that emphasises academic excellence, interdisciplinary learning, self-understanding, creativity and integrity. The average class size is 6:1. In addition to traditional academic subjects, student-initiated projects, critical thinking skills, nature education, outdoor activities and practical skills are encouraged.

Description: A co-educational boarding school founded by the educator and philosopher, J. Krishnamurti. It has students from over twenty countries and is set on 40 acres of rolling countryside. Because of its size the school feels like a large family rather than a boarding school. Meals are vegetarian, freshly prepared from mainly organically-grown produce. The aim of the school is to explore life in the light of Krishnamurti's teachings on the transformation of human consciousness.

First year at Brockwood

I came to Brockwood Park School as a result of my parents' interest in the founder, J. Krishnamurti. In 1995, my father had visited the school, spent a lot of time with the students, and came home fascinated. As soon as I was old enough, I came to spend a week in the school as a prospective student. In that week I was introduced to an entirely new world.

The first thing I noticed was the size of the school. I had known that Brockwood was made up of only about a hundred people; however seeing them all sitting together in one room made it seem more like a big family rather than a group of people coming from over twenty-seven cultures, all of different ages and with different ideas and beliefs.

The diversity of the people attending the school does not prevent it from creating its own culture. Brockwood culture shapes people just as any other culture does. After being here for seven months many of my opinions, prejudices, and general ideas have changed drastically. Though some would say that Brockwood's culture is created only by the people who live here, I feel that the beauty of the place itself exudes a sort of magical energy that influences all of us and plays a role in the creation of its culture.

At Brockwood we are constantly reminded to take a questioning approach to what we see and hear. Many ideas and concepts that I have never even thought about before become major topics for discussion. Inquiry Time, a weekly class when all students and teachers come together, is constructed around philosophical topics that come up in our daily life. It differs from other classes in that nobody is teaching or even leading the class, but an atmosphere suitable for open discussion is created. Themes vary from the very general, such as 'fear' or 'appearance', to the more specific, like the intentions of hip-hop music. Often when we discuss such topics as a school we start to become aware of the beliefs and values which underlie our opinions and habits. This may happen immediately or after several weeks, and sometimes, without even noticing how it happened, people find that their outlook on things has changed.

Though Brockwood holds us to academic demands, many of the valuable new lessons we get come from the people around us. There is not a big division between staff and students so it becomes easier to come to know each other and develop friendships with teachers.

This is both one of the strongest and one of the most fragile environments I have ever been a part of. Every day I am reminded of the impact just one person can make on a place. However, it is held together by a clear sense of purpose, care for the students, and a willingness to listen and to change. Though Brockwood Park has experienced its fair share of ordeals it remains the richest cultural and intellectual melting pot I have ever found myself in the midst of.

Kathy Slivinskaya, ex-student, Brockwood Park School

Figure 6.1 Time for reflection.
Credit: Dharma School and Tim Page Photography

The Dharma School
The White House, 149 Ladies Mile Road, Patcham, Brighton
BN1 8TB
Tel: 01273 502055   Fax: 01273 556580
Website: www.users.computerweekly.net/dharmaschool

School established: 1994

Age range of pupils: 3–11

Maximum number of pupils: 70

Number of staff: 4 teachers, 4 learning support assistants, 1 caretaker, 1 bursar

Curriculum: Follows the National Curriculum but does not undertake SATs tests. Small classes, some negotiation of curriculum with children.

Description: The Dharma School is the first primary school in the UK to be based on Buddhist principles. It provides a thorough and integrated curriculum compatible with the National Curriculum. Includes periods for daily reflection and focuses on the spiritual quality of human life. The school building is a 1930s detached house in a garden with natural and created play areas. All teaching staff are fully qualified with experience in mainstream education as well as having a Buddhist practice.

King Alfred's School
North End Road, London NW11 7HY
Tel: 0208 457 5200   Fax: 0208 457 5264
Email: KAS@Kingalfred.barnet.sch.uk
Website: www.kingalfred.barnet.sch.uk

School established: 1898

Age range of pupils: 4–18

Maximum number of pupils: 500

Number of staff: 75

Exams offered: GCSE, A/S level, A level

Curriculum: Subjects offered include music, technology, Spanish, photography and information and communication technology

Description: This co-educational, independent day school was well ahead of its time when it was founded. It is still co-educational, all age, secular and embraces a wide ability range. Provides a rigorous academic education for all and has very good examination results despite its non-selective policy. The school encourages all aspects of a child's development from the early years in the lower school to sixth formers being offered responsibilities such as membership of the pupils' council or even the governing body. Particular emphasis is placed on the need to research and to work independently and to play a full part in the life of the school.

St Christopher's School
Letchworth, Hertfordshire SG6 3JZ
Tel: 01462 679301   Fax: 01462 481578
Email: stchris.admin@vmplc.co.uk
Website: www.stchris.co.uk

School established: 1915

Age range of pupils: 2–19

Maximum number of pupils: 600

Number of staff: 135

Curriculum: Full curriculum from Montessori nursery through to 21 subjects available at AS/A level

Description: Since 1915 the school has encouraged children to express themselves, to listen to others and to feel that they are world citizens. There is a strong sense of community. The houses for younger boarders have a homely feel while seniors live in student-style rooms. Day pupils share in the evening and weekend life, making use of the facilities for technology and the creative arts. There is no compulsory worship and no uniform. The diet is vegetarian. The aim is for our young people to be competent and confident, to have courage and initiative, to make friends and find the fun in life.

Sunrise Primary School
55 Coniston Road, London N17 0EX
Tel: 0208 885 3354 Fax: 0208 806 6279

School established: 1991

Age range of pupils: 2½–11

Maximum number of pupils: 45

Number of staff: 3 teachers, 2 assistants

Curriculum: Curriculum based upon the principles of neo-humanist education. Traditional subjects are interlinked through unifying themes. Creativity, life skills, character development, morality and meditation are also considered important.

Description: Aims to develop every child towards his or her highest potential by educating all aspects of their physical, emotional, intellectual, creative, intuitional and spiritual being. This holistic approach extends to nurturing in each child an understanding of, and love for, the universal whole to which each of us belongs.

Midlands

Accelerated Tutorial School
45 Church Road, Edgbaston, Birmingham B15 3SW
Tel: 0121 454 5787

School established: 1999

Age range of pupils: 6–16

Maximum number of pupils: 120

Curriculum: National and personalised

Description: Small, multicultural co-educational school working towards and beyond the National Curriculum. There are accelerated programmes to accommodate individual pupils' strengths.

North West

Maharishi School
Cobbs Brow Lane, Lathom, Lancashire L40 6JJ
Tel: 01695 729912   Fax: 01695 729030
Email: enquiries@maharishischool.com
Website: www.maharishischool.com

School established: 1986

Age range of pupils: 4–16

Maximum number of pupils: 120

Number of staff: 16

Curriculum: Covers the conventional academic areas

Description: Through the approach of Maharishi's consciousness-based education, students not only learn the traditional academic disciplines but experience the growth of their own consciousness, the basis of the whole learning process. Aims to provide students with a natural way to develop their full creative potential in all areas of life.

Scotland

Sathya Sai School
20 The Scores, St Andrews, Fife KY16 9AS
Tel: 01334 477384

School established: 2001

Age range of pupils: 3–11

Maximum number of pupils: 20

Curriculum: Based on a Montessori approach

Description: The school is based on the teachings of the Indian social reformer, Sri Sathya Sai Baba, and aims to provide a holistic learning environment to support children's growth at all levels – physical, emotional, intellectual and spiritual. In association with Scottish Natural Heritage it runs a nature school twice a week for all pupils.

Further reading

Young, M. (1988) 'Choice in Education', *Resurgence*, 130: September/ October.

John Dewey

Dewey, J. (1900) *School and Society*, Chicago: University of Chicago Press.
Dewey, J. (1916) *Democracy and Education*, New York: Macmillan.
Dewey, J. (1938) *Experience and Education*, London: Collier Macmillan.

Grundtvig and the Danish Free Schools

Powell, R. (2001) *The Danish Free School Tradition*, Kelso: Curlew.

Freinet

Freinet, C. (1993 – originally published 1949) *Education through Work*, New York: Edwin Mellen Press.
Freinet, C. (1990) 'Cooperative Learning and Social Change' in D. Clandfield, and J. Sivell, (eds) *Selected Writings of Célestin Freinet*, Toronto: OISE Press.
Lee, W. B. (1994) *Freinet Pedagogy – Theory and Practice*, New York: Edwin Mellen Press.

Reggio Emilia

Edwards, C., Foreman, G. and Gandini, L. (1998) *The Hundred Languages of Children*, Conneticut: Ablex.

For information

Grundtvig and the Danish Free Schools

Friskolernes Kontor
Prices Havevej 11
DK 5600 Fåborg
Denmark
Tel: 0045 6261 3013
Fax: 0045 6261 3911
www.friskoler.dk

Jenaplan

Nederlanse Jenaplan Vereniging
Rembrandtlaan 50
1741 KJ Schagen
The Netherlands

Tel: 0031 224 213306
Fax: 0031 224 213043
Email: Jenaplanbureau@hetnet.nl
Website: www.jenaplan.nl

Freinet

Institut Coopératif de l'Ecole Moderne
18 rue Sarrazin
F-44000 Nantes
France
Tel: 0033 2 40 89 47 50
Fax: 0033 2 40 47 16 91

Pädagogik-Kooperative
Goebenstrasse 8
D-28209 Bremen
Germany
Tel: 0049 421 34 49 29
Website: www.freinet.org

Reggio Emilia

Reggio Children
Piazza della Vittoria
6-42100 Reggio Emilia
Italy
Tel: 0039 0522 455416
Email: info@reggio-children.it

Sightlines Initiative
20 Great North Road
Newcastle upon Tyne
NE2 4PS
Tel: 0191 261 7666
Email: info@sightlines-initiative.com
Website: www.sightlines-initiative.com

Part 2

Doing it yourself

Chapter 7

Setting up a small school or learning centre

It is better to light a candle than curse the darkness.

motto of The Small School at Hartland

In recent years increasing interest in the idea of setting up a school or learning centre has been shown by parents and teachers wishing to explore different approaches to education. For parents who reject mainstream schooling but who have no alternative schools in their area it offers a third option. For teachers who feel that they cannot teach effectively within the constraints of the state system it enables them to put their own educational philosophy into practice. As for children – many appear to thrive in small learning communities in which they are each known and valued as individuals.

Setting up a new educational project is a challenge. It is a completely legal option and the government publishes guidelines covering the legal requirements. It takes a lot of time, energy and commitment – but it can be done and this chapter lays out the key elements in the process and gives guidance on how to go about it.

The main stages are:

- Getting started
- Finding a building
- Setting up a charity
- Establishing a company
- Finding teachers
- Registering with the Department for Education and Skills
- Raising funds
- Agreeing management structures
- Working with parents and the local community

- Deciding on the curriculum and exams
- Buying furniture and equipment.

Getting started

The project is most likely to be successful if a small group of people work together – it may be a group of friends. Alternatively an open and well-advertised meeting can be held to gauge the local interest for such a project and to form an initial steering group.

Once this group has been formed a series of meetings can be held to discuss what the school or learning centre will be like and to reach a broad consensus on key issues. Questions for consideration include:

- What is the purpose of the project?
- What will the children learn?
- Will the project follow any particular educational philosophy? (Steiner, Montessori, Dewey etc.)
- What will the age range be?
- Will attendance be compulsory?
- Will part-time attendance be allowed?
- Will the National Curriculum be followed?
- Will there be tests or exams?
- How will the project be funded? Will it charge fees?
- How big will it be?
- Will it take children with special educational needs? If so, how many?
- How will the project be managed?

It can take time to create a shared vision and this may involve people leaving the group and others joining. Just because people are dissatisfied with mainstream education it does not mean that they will agree about what an alternative should be like. There are many different ways to organise an educational project and the first section of this book gives some idea of the range. A new school does not have to subscribe to any particular educational philosophy but may instead focus on being an environmental school, a democratic school or a creative school. Its main aim may be to involve parents and the local community. It may be set up for children with a specific educational need – for dyslexics or for emotionally disturbed children, for example. It may contain elements of all of these: there is much room for debate. It is sometimes the case that one person has a strong vision and other people join in with that.

It is advisable to limit the amount of time spent discussing the philosophy as such a debate can continue indefinitely. What happens in practice will depend very much on the teachers who are appointed. It is advisable therefore to make progress on the practicalities of the project to keep the momentum going.

One way to proceed is to set up a sub-group for each of the main tasks. These include:

- Finding premises
- Raising funds
- Appointing staff
- Establishing a charitable trust.

It is worth giving the project a name and producing an initial publicity leaflet early on. This gives the project an identity and helps to raise awareness of it locally. There is a considerable body of research (much of it American) which makes the case for small schools and small classes which will help in drawing up publicity materials and making the case for funding. This research can be accessed via Human Scale Education's website at www.hse.org.uk

Finding a building

There are a number of considerations to be taken into account when looking for a building. These include:

- Urban or rural, town centre or outskirts
- Cost
- Accessibility – is there public transport?
- Is land needed with the building? (for outside activities, growing food etc.)
- Health and safety regulations
- Fire regulations
- Storage space.

Thought must be given to what the building is wanted for and how much space will be needed. For some activities such as sport, outside facilities can be used.

It is advisable to rent a building rather than buy one, at least in the first instance. Contact can be made with the council, housing associations, estate agents, local universities and colleges to find out whether they have any available buildings which could be used. There may be an empty and disused school for example which could be ideal. Failing this, domestic rather than business premises may be more suitable as they have a number of smaller rooms. The lease must be carefully studied. It is also important to look carefully at the likely running costs of any building.

If the aim is to buy a building, there are different ways of raising the finance – by applying for grants from charitable trusts, taking out a mortgage from a bank or raising donations from supporters. There is also the possibility of setting up a share system whereby shares in the building are sold to friends and supporters.

If the chosen building was not used as a school previously, planning permission for change of use is needed. This can be problematic in a residential area, particularly if there is opposition to the project.

Some projects start off very small in a person's home or in a church or community hall. However, once there are five children attending full time there is a legal requirement to be registered with the Department for Education and Skills and this brings with it implications for the building in terms of fire and health and safety regulations.

The requirements which are laid out in the *Education (School Premises) Regulations* 1996 stipulate:

• The number of toilets needed
• A separate staff toilet
• Changing accommodation to include showers at secondary level
• A room for medical examinations and for the care of sick pupils
• A room for teachers to work in
• Storage space
• Appropriate space for the preparation of food
• Adequate lighting and heating.

There are also requirements relating to ventilation, water supplies and drainage.

Additional requirements relating to fire regulations refer to the number of exits, the need for fire doors and fireproofing, fire extinguishing and alarm systems as well as fire resistance capacity. Before taking on a building it is essential to have it inspected by the local Fire Officer to determine whether these regulations can be complied with.

Insurance will be required for the building and contents as well as public liability insurance.

Setting up a charity and a company

Registration as a charity is advisable as it has a number of advantages. It enables the project to raise funds from the public and from grant-making trusts, to pay reduced business rates on premises and to obtain tax relief on donations made by covenant and by gift aid.

The Charity Commission produces an information pack on *Starting a Charity and Applying for Registration* which lays out the procedure for registration. A governing document needs to be drawn up to set out what the charity does and how it will operate. This has to contain information about the aims of the charity, its powers, the trustees, meetings of trustees, membership, accounts, land and investments and dissolution. The Charity Commission has model governing documents which can be used as a basis and it is advisable to follow one of these as closely as possible to minimise the delay in becoming registered.

There are three different ways in which a charity can operate – as an unincorporated association, as a trust or as a company. A decision about this can be made on the basis of how the project is to be run and the Charity Commission will give advice. Setting up an unincorporated association is the most straightforward of these options. However there is an advantage in setting up a company which is incorporated and is thus a legal entity in its own right, separate from members and directors; it means that there is limited liability in case of debt. Projects which are set up as companies need to register with Companies House. They are likely also to need help with drawing up the governing document from either a solicitor or from the National Council for Voluntary Organisations.

Trustees are responsible for the management of the charity and should be chosen carefully. Their responsibilities include running the charity (although this can be delegated to staff), keeping proper accounts and ensuring that assets are used for the purposes for which they were intended and the upkeep of any property belonging to the charity. It is important that meetings are minuted and records are kept to protect the charity from allegations of mismanagement.

The National Council for Voluntary Organisations offers advice to charities and will assist in the process of becoming registered for a fee.

Registering with the Department for Education and Skills

Independent schools are required to register with the Department for Education and Skills if they are providing full-time education for five or more pupils of compulsory school age. An application form and information pack containing *Guidance for Proprietors* is available from the DfES Independent Schools Team. The application form needs to be returned within a month of the school opening. A criminal background check of staff has to be carried out to ensure that those who are employed have not previously been barred from working with children.

The DfES will register the school provisionally on receipt of the application form. Final registration is not granted until the school has been inspected to ensure that minimum standards are being met.

The school will be visited by Her Majesty's Inspectors of Schools (HMI) who will look at premises, staffing and teaching. The Inspector will report informally to the head teacher and a report will be sent to the Registrar of Independent Schools. This document will be used as a basis for judging suitability for registration. If registration is not approved the school will be told what is needed to satisfy minimum requirements. A repeat visit will be made by the inspectors to check that their recommendations have been put into place before final registration can take place.

Standards in independent schools are expected to be broadly comparable with those in maintained schools. Whilst such schools are not required to teach the National Curriculum they are expected to offer a broad and balanced curriculum in order to keep open as many options as possible for their students in terms of future education, training and employment.

The school will be required by the DfES to keep a register of admissions and a daily attendance register. There are no requirements in terms of the number of sessions or the hours of attendance, but if schools broadly follow local authority or other independent schools in the area this will be acceptable.

Independent schools are bound by the *Health and Safety at Work Act 1974*, the *Sex Discrimination Act 1975*, the *Race Relations Act 1976* and the *Food Hygiene Regulations 1970* as well as the relevant provisions of business/charity and employment law, all of which are published by HMSO.

If the school caters mainly for children with statements of special educational needs (SEN), advice should be sought from the DfES as inspection procedures are different. Relevant information is available from the DfES SEN Independent Schools Team.

Finding teachers

The most critical factor in the success of a small school or learning centre is the staff, who must be chosen with extreme care. Teachers must be able to inspire and motivate children and it is likely that they will need to be able to teach across several subject areas.

A major aim of small schools is to tailor the education to suit each child and this requires different skills from mainstream education. Instead of teachers who are practised at delivering lessons to groups of thirty children or so, the school is more likely to want staff who are able to discover the interests and talents of each child and work outwards from this point. The role is more one of mentor and coach and will undoubtedly require staff who are prepared to accept pastoral responsibilities alongside their teaching role. Other qualities to look for include imagination, creativity, flexibility, ability to work cooperatively, interpersonal skills, commitment and a natural empathy with children.

A teaching qualification is not a legal requirement in independent schools but it is advisable to employ some qualified staff. Appointments should not be rushed into. It is better not to appoint than to appoint the wrong person, as such initiatives are heavily dependent on the quality of their staff and the wrong appointment can destroy a project. It is a good idea to have a probationary period to allow time to see whether a new teacher is suitable.

Contracts including details of grievance procedures will need to be drawn up. Help with this can be sought from the local ACAS office (details of which can be found in the telephone directory).

Rates of pay are generally considerably lower in alternative schools than in the maintained or conventional independent sector, but this is often made up for by job satisfaction. Salaries should take account of the cost of living in the locality. Some part-time staff may work voluntarily.

Thought must be given to how to be a good employer so that staff can get the most out of their job and give of their best. This involves being clear about who staff are responsible to, having good lines of communication and giving adequate support.

Raising the funds

There are a number of ways in which to raise the funds to set up and run a school and these include:

* Statutory funding
* Grants from charitable trusts

- Donations from individuals or businesses
- Charging fees
- Setting up a business
- Local Exchange Trading Scheme (LETS).

Statutory funding

The majority of alternative schools do not receive any funding from the state and therefore charge fees to cover most or all of their running costs. Whilst these fees are often kept as low as possible – to cover costs rather than to generate profit – they inevitably exclude many families who are unable to pay. This means that alternative schools are often seen as elitist, which is certainly not their intention, but is rather a consequence of the government's unpreparedness to finance different kinds of education.

Over the past twenty years only one school in the UK based on an alternative philosophy has been able to procure ongoing public funding (although there are cases of individual children being funded by their local authority). Recent legislation has devolved responsibility for the funding of new schools to local education authorities (LEAs), so people who wish to set up a school must contact their LEA to make an application. The decision as to whether to fund a new school is taken by the Schools Organisation Committee. Making an application involves a lengthy process of demonstrating demand for the school and producing a business plan – but in the long term such schools will be more financially viable and sustainable and accessible to all if they are publicly funded.

There is a catch, however. Schools funded by the LEA are currently required to teach the National Curriculum, but it is the narrowness and prescriptiveness of the National Curriculum which is stimulating demand for alternative approaches to education. Some existing alternative schools say that they are able to meet National Curriculum targets; new schools may not wish to do this. For exemption from the National Curriculum an application has to be made directly to the Secretary of State for Education.

The question of statutory funding for alternative schools is currently under review by the government, so there is a case for pressing the issue to demonstrate the demand for alternatives.

Funding from charitable trusts

New projects can apply to charitable trusts for grants towards setting up costs. Raising money from this source for ongoing running costs is more difficult.

There are a number of reference books which list trusts including the *Directory of Grant Making Trusts* (Charities Aid Foundation) and *The Guide to Major Trusts Volumes 1 and 2* (Fitzherbert and Richards, 2001). The Charities Aid Foundation publishes *Trust Fundraising* (Clay 1999), which gives useful advice on how to approach trusts.

It is important to research trusts carefully and apply only to those whose criteria fit the project. It is worthwhile phoning the trust (if they accept telephone enquiries) before making an application to discuss the project, to find out when the next trustees' meeting is, how much to apply for and what aspect of the work to apply for.

It is advisable not to send too much information: a brief letter explaining what the project is and what the money is needed for, with supporting information attached, should suffice. Trusts will want to see financial projections and so it is important to draw up a financial plan. If anyone connected with the project knows the trustee of any trust it is a good idea to make a personal approach as such approaches are generally the most successful.

If a trust agrees to make a grant it should be kept informed of the progress of the project by sending regular reports and inviting trustees to visit.

Donations from individuals or businesses

Individuals and local businesses can be approached for support. Funding from large companies is generally difficult to secure (and may, in any case, not be welcome on ethical grounds). It is important that the publicity material is well produced as this generates greater confidence in the project. If donors can be persuaded to covenant donations over four years, the tax on their gift can be reclaimed from the Inland Revenue.

Parental contributions/fees

If the school is non-fee-paying voluntary contributions from parents can be sought. Parents can agree collectively to raise a percentage of the school's costs. One way is for families to contribute what they can individually and for the balance to be raised by the group as a whole through fund-raising. Parents who cannot contribute in cash can contribute in other ways by donating goods which the school requires or by giving their time. In this way, nobody who wishes to send a child to the school is excluded.

If on the other hand the school decides to charge fees in order to cover its costs, these can be banded so that people pay according to how much they earn and how many children they have at the school. There is also the possibility of raising funding from trusts for a bursary fund so that families who cannot afford the fees are still able to send their child.

In order to reduce costs projects can maximise the amount of voluntary help they use from parents and from supportive members of the local community. Children can take responsibility for cleaning the school and can also cook lunch on a rota basis, with a parent or member of staff.

Setting up a business

One way of insuring a regular income is by setting up a business alongside the school and diverting all the profits. Several small schools have raised income by operating a fee-paying nursery. There are also cases of shops being run by parents to assist with funding the school. This can be very time consuming, though, and it takes double the effort to establish two successful ventures, when one is quite hard enough!

Local Exchange Trading Scheme – LETS

If there is a LETS scheme in the area the project can join this and trade goods and services with other members of the community without using money. There are many ways in which schools can benefit from involvement in such schemes, from letting their building and accepting parental contributions in the local currency to buying in teacher time and specialist skills.

Agreeing management structures

There are a number of different ways of running a school and this will depend in part on the trust deed. It is likely that there will be a board of trustees, like a governing body. The extent to which this group makes the decisions can vary depending on the priorities of the school. It can be a rubber stamping group which hands over the day-to-day running to a different group – such as teachers and students or parents and teachers – or to a group with representatives from the teacher, parent, student and trustee body. Alternatively the trustee group can retain responsibility for the main decisions.

There may be a desire to work as a cooperative; however it is not possible to register officially as a cooperative and as a charity. Cooperatives are established for the benefit of their members and this is the direct opposite of charities, which have to be set up with wider purposes.

Most alternative schools aim to be democratic but this principle can be put into practice in different ways. Some schools appoint a head who has overall responsibility as far as the day-to-day running of the school is involved. Other schools have a cooperative body of teachers with no head and they share responsibility. In some schools the parents play a major role in decision-making; in others it is the students, in conjunction with staff, who make decisions at a regular meeting. In some schools everything is decided by voting; in others the aim is to achieve a consensus.

There is no one right way, but perhaps the golden rule should be that anyone who is going to be affected by a decision should be able to participate in making it.

Deciding on the curriculum and exams

Independent schools are not legally obliged to follow the National Curriculum. This gives them the freedom to develop their own curricula and this is one of the greatest benefits. The school inspectors will suggest that an eye is kept on the National Curriculum but this is entirely optional.

Some projects will decide what they want the focus of the curriculum to be before the school opens. Some may want an emphasis on environmental sustainability, so that the curriculum and the running of the school are underpinned by ecological issues. Other projects may be based on the centrality of the arts to learning so that the curriculum is explored through music, dance, drama, art and crafts. A further option is to involve the students in designing the curriculum so that it reflects their interests. Some schools offer a range of courses and students sign up for those which they are interested in attending.

Since one of the main reasons for establishing an alternative school is to be better able to meet the needs of each child, it is helpful to draw up an individual learning plan for each child in consultation with the child and possibly the parents as well so that the child has an input into decisions about what, how, where and when he or she is learning.

If the school is applying for statutory funding it will need to follow the National Curriculum and carry out the associated tests (SATs) unless exemption has been granted by the Secretary of State for Education. Information about the National Curriculum is available from the Qualifications and Curriculum Authority (QCA).

Secondary schools generally offer GCSE courses to their students. Details of courses are available from the different examination boards and schools can decide which syllabus is most appropriate for their situation. By registering as an examination centre students can take their GCSEs at the school. Alternatively they can be entered as external candidates elsewhere.

Schools do not need to feel pressured into encouraging students to take nine or ten GCSEs as is the norm in many schools. In fact only five are required for acceptance on to higher education courses. Some alternative schools reduce the pressure on students by encouraging them to take a smaller number spread over two or even three years. Taking this approach does not necessarily mean that students study fewer subjects. Instead time is freed up for students to study subjects they are interested in, in a way that is not dictated by exam courses. It also opens the way to a more cross-curricular approach.

Buying furniture and equipment

Much of the furniture and equipment that is needed can be bought second hand but it is important to have things of reasonable quality. Schools get a lot of wear and tear and equipment needs to be able to stand up to this. Furthermore, what the school looks like and how it is decorated makes a statement about the values of the school community. Many state schools are in a poor state of repair and this can give the message that the pupils are not important. We know that people are affected by their environment and care should be taken in how the school is fitted out in order to create a positive atmosphere.

Many local authorities have their own educational suppliers which offer good value and schools may be able to access such a service. If a list of what is needed is produced and circulated it is likely that some things will be donated.

Some of the items which may be needed initially include:

• Tables and chairs

- Telephone and fax
- Shelving
- Books
- Photocopier
- Paper
- Blackboards/whiteboards
- Science equipment
- Sports equipment
- Musical instruments
- Arts and crafts equipment
- Computers
- Television and video.

Working with parents and the local community

It is likely that parents of prospective students will be closely involved in setting up the project. Once it opens it is necessary to be clear about what their role will be. Many parents become involved in such a project because they want closer involvement in their child's education. In some alternative schools parents are involved in decision-making at all levels of school life whereas other schools have found that it works better if the parents as a body are not closely involved with the day-to-day running of the school, leaving this to the teaching staff.

Parents may assist with teaching and curriculum design, also with fund-raising, transportation, administration, classroom support and cleaning. A decision will have to be made as to whether they should be paid to teach. It can be divisive if some parents are paid to teach while others are not paid for different kinds of jobs.

It helps if there is a clear line of communication between teachers and parents in connection with the child's progress, so that parents can support the child's learning. Regular parents' meetings to discuss issues of common interest and individual consultations so that parents are kept informed of their child's progress and any difficulties are important. In a small school, teachers can know the child's family and home situation and this can help with understanding the child.

As far as the local community is concerned, alternative schools, by virtue of their size, are well placed to work with the community, sharing resources and skills. The school can use the resources of the community – the library and sports centre for example – and make available its own resources – space for evening groups and perhaps some classes. In this way a positive relationship between the project and the local community can be established.

Cooperation can go much further than this. The local environment and local people can be used as a resource much more easily than in a large school. Small schools can take advantage of the opportunities for learning provided beyond the school grounds because their size gives them greater flexibility. Groups can go out of school to do environmental projects or to do community work. Much thought needs to be given to how schools can take advantage of this potential to ensure that children's learning is based on their experiences with real places, real people and real issues. Such an approach enables communities to play an active role in the education of their young people and for young people to make a significant contribution to their local communities.

For information

Charities Commission
St Albans House
57–60 Haymarket
London SW1Y 4QX
Tel: 0207 210 4548

Department for Education and Skills
(Independent Schools Team)
Mowden Hall
Darlington
DL3 9BG
Tel: 01325 460155

HMSO
PO Box 276
London SW8 5DT
Tel: 0207 873 9090

Human Scale Education
Unit 8
Fairseat Farm
Chew Stoke
Bristol
BS40 8XF
Tel: 01275 332516
Website: www.hse.org.uk

National Council for Voluntary Organisations (NCVO)
Regents Wharf
8 All Saints Street
London
N1 9RL
Tel: 0207 713 6161

Qualifications and Curriculum Authority (QCA)
29 Bolton Street
London
W1Y 7PD
Tel: 0207 509 5555
Website: www.open.gov.uk/qca

Further reading

Carnie, F. (1999) *Setting up a Small School*, Bath: Human Scale Education.
Charities Aid Foundation (2001) *Directory of Grant Making Trusts*, Kent: CAF.
Clay, A. (ed.) (1999) *Trust Fundraising*, West Malling: Charities Aid Foundation.
Croall, J. (1997) *LETS Act Locally*, London: Gulbenkian Foundation.
Fitzherbert, L. and Richards, G. (2001) *The Guide to Major Trusts*, London: Directory of Social Change.

Chapter 8

Home-based education

> Schools have not necessarily much to do with education ... they are mainly institutions of control where certain basic habits must be instilled in the young. Education is quite different and has little place in school.
>
> Winston Churchill

It is estimated that more than 20,000 (and possibly as many as 50,000) children are now being educated at home in the UK. This movement started with a few pioneering families in the 1950s and has grown exponentially, helped by the growth in computer technology which has made it much easier for families to access information and support.

A variety of reasons lead families to the decision to home educate. Some parents of children who have been bullied at school have decided that their children will do better in a secure and supportive home environment. There are many instances in which parents of children with special educational needs believe that those needs are not being catered for at school and have decided that they could do a better job at home. In cases where children are just plain bored, frustrated or unhappy at school parents have felt that it was counterproductive to continue to send them.

On the other hand, some parents decide long before their children reach school age that they do not want to send them to school. A range of reasons are given for this decision – they may believe that there is too much concentration on formal learning at school, or that the child's creativity will be stifled, or that children are better motivated to learn if they can choose what to study, or that it is unnatural for children to be cooped up in a class with thirty other children of the same age.

Whatever the reason behind the decision to home educate, in the vast majority of cases it is not taken lightly. Some parents come to the decision very quickly, catapulted by some unhappy event at school. The majority, however, often spend months or even years weighing up the pros and cons before taking the plunge.

It is not an easy decision to make because of the impact on the whole family. It is a huge commitment for parents in terms of time and energy and one major consequence is the reduction in the wage-earning capacity. The fact that a growing number of families are choosing this option demonstrates the depth of feeling about the inadequacies of the education system and the sacrifices parents are prepared to make for the sake of their children's well-being.

Home education and the law

The first question often asked about home-based education is 'Is it legal?' The 1996 Education Act and the 1944 Education Act before it stated unequivocally that it is. The 1996 Education Act states that:

> The parent of every child of compulsory school age shall cause him to receive efficient full-time education suitable to his age, ability and aptitude and to any special educational needs he may have, either by regular attendance at school or otherwise.

The legislation makes two things clear – first that education is the responsibility of parents and second, that it can happen at school *or otherwise*. (This clause was the inspiration for the name of the first support organisation for home educators, Education Otherwise, which was founded in the 1970s.)

This legislation is reinforced by the European Convention on Human Rights (1989) which states that:

> No person shall be denied the right to education. In the exercise of any functions which it assumes in relation to education and to
> · teaching, the State shall respect the right of parents to ensure such education and teaching is in conformity with their own religious and philosophical convictions.

In spite of the legislation local education authorities all respond differently to home-educating families. Whilst some are supportive and others are tolerant, a minority are hostile and can make life difficult.

Parents need to be clear that whilst it is their right to home educate they may be required by their local authority to prove that the education which they provide is appropriate to the child's age, ability and aptitude and that it is efficient and full-time. This can, of course, be interpreted very broadly and allows for a variety of approaches. It may however be in parents' interests to write down the reasons for their decision to home educate, their philosophy and how they go about it in order to satisfy the local authority that they are taking their responsibilities seriously. Local authority officials may wish to visit the family to assess the situation. Families who are new to home education would be well advised to make contact with other home-educating families in their area, to find out what the approach of the authority is likely to be so that they can prepare themselves in the best possible way.

There is no obligation to inform the LEA and it is a decision for the family whether or not to do so. If the child has never been to school or been registered for a school, the authority has no way of knowing that the family is home educating unless it is informed by the family itself or some other party. However if the child has been registered with a school it is the duty of the parents to ask for the child to be taken off the register, and at this stage the school is required to inform the education authority. If they fail to do so the local authority can prosecute parents for not sending their child to school.

If a local authority is concerned that a child is not receiving adequate education it can require parents to show that they are fulfilling their duties. If the authority is not satisfied it can issue a school attendance order requiring parents to send their child to school.

Parents who are having difficulties with their LEA are advised to contact the home education organisations for advice, and failing this, contact a solicitor specialising in education law. Having said this, the majority of families do not have significant difficulties in this respect. As home educating becomes more common, local authorities, on the whole, are becoming more cooperative in the way they liaise with families who have chosen this path.

Getting started

The first thing you need to know is that you do not need to be a teacher to educate your child at home. Furthermore you do not have to teach the National Curriculum. Many people are put off by the thought that they have no experience of teaching and they would not know where to begin with the National Curriculum, but neither is necessary.

There are many different ways of approaching home education, and as with all education there is no one right way to do it. Different approaches suit different children and families at different times. At one end of the spectrum there is a completely formal approach where a school-like environment is recreated in the home. Parents draw up a timetable and the different subjects are studied much as they would be studied at school.

At the other end of the spectrum is an autonomous approach to learning whereby children choose what they are going to learn and how and when they are going to learn it. The parents follow the lead of the child and give support and assistance as and when requested.

In reality the majority of families probably find themselves at different places along this continuum at different times. Different topics and themes lend themselves to being learned in different ways and the most successful home educators are likely to be those who are the most flexible in their approach. It takes time and a good deal of trial and error for families to discover what works in their own situation.

A good first step is to contact the different home education organisations (listed at the end of this chapter). A wealth of information is

Figure 8.1 Home-educated children, Anume and Ollie, learning the glockenspiel.

Credit: Terri Dowty

now available to help families who have chosen this route. There is a range of books, resources, regular magazines and websites all giving advice and support.

The next step might be to make contact with other home-educating families in the area. One of the greatest concerns of parents who decide to home educate is that the experience might be socially isolating for their children. Whilst many families have testified otherwise, saying that their children become adept at mixing with a wider range of people than they would ever meet in school, it is reassuring to meet up with others who have chosen the same path. The main support organisations provide lists of members by area. In many areas informal groups have been set up so that families meet up on a regular basis. Such groups might organise activities for children or arrange trips or outings. They might pool the resources of the parents so that different parents offer to teach and support children within their own field of expertise. In some areas families have set up a learning centre and these are listed at the end of the chapter.

Another step would be to find out what resources are available within the community. There are likely to be many local resources which can be tapped into. Libraries, museums, sports centres, parks, zoos, community centres, theatres and local colleges are just a few of the places which offer learning opportunities and resources. One of the many strengths of a home-based approach to learning is that it can take place in a wide variety of settings and can be much more active and participative than is normally the case at school. Quite spontaneously families can go and look at bridges, rivers, canals, farms, old buildings, new buildings, shops, factories, the seaside. Learning experiences are easily woven into everyday life: cooking, gardening, shopping, visits to the doctor, appointments with plumbers/electricians/builders all offer an opportunity to learn. Television and radio have a wide range of educational programmes for schools and for the Open University, details of which are available from the BBC.

These are some starting points, but the most important starting point of all is the child. Find out what the child is interested in and begin there. A motivated and engaged child will learn infinitely more than a child who is studying something against her will. And if you start with what seems like a very narrow subject area be assured that if the child is truly engaged, whatever subject it is can be opened out to encompass a range of skills and a greater breadth of subject areas than was originally imagined. Let go of the idea that the child has to learn English, maths, science, history, geography and other subjects in any kind of structured way. Whilst this is possible and at times desirable, for example in preparing for any exams, one of the benefits of home educating is that learning does not have to be divided into subject boxes. A more holistic and cross-curricular approach is well suited to home-based learning and can help children to make sense of their world.

Home education – one family's approach

When I'm asked what kind of 'approach' we use to home education, I never quite know what to answer. Chaotic? That's probably how it seems from outside and, sometimes, from inside as well. All I can say is that, whatever it's called, it works!

After five years of this, we've relaxed into an easygoing relationship where days take their course and 'work' is a meaningless term. That's not to say it doesn't happen; sometimes, when I look back over a day I'm astonished at just how much ground the boys have covered, but separating out the day's components into work or not-work would be quite impossible.

Let's take yesterday. We were slow to get up. The boys were tired from a late night at the theatre, seeing *Julius Caesar* with their dad, and stayed in bed reading, which gave me the chance to catch up on some work.

A sound like machine-gun fire told me that my 9-year-old demon percussionist was up and practising, so I gave my attention to his older brother, who needed to write a book review for a magazine. In return, he wrote some webpages for me. I drank my coffee, looking over his shoulder in disbelief as he turned out pages of inexplicable symbols, wondering, as I so often do, how on earth he learned to write this weird language, let alone touch-type – something I've never mastered.

Having produced enough squiggles and dots, he replaced his younger brother in what we laughingly call 'the lounge' – actually so full with gradually accumulated instruments that there's only room for a single armchair – and settled down to play his harp. Meanwhile, just for fun, I ran a simultaneous equation, which somebody had put up on the home education Internet list, past my drummer boy, curious to see what he would make of it. (Perhaps I should explain that his greatest passion after music is probably maths.)

He stared at it for a while, shaking his head as I hinted ineffectually at a way of starting off. I looked around the room for a 'visual aid' and, in a flash of inspiration, seized the fruit bowl. If a satsuma equals two apples, and a satsuma also equals one apple and two bananas, what else are two apples equal to? Aha! I love that look, and my own sense of relief, when light dawns.

We wandered down to the forest for a walk, picking up a newspaper en route. As we walked, we talked about debtors' prisons and suffragettes, Cuba and the Bay of Pigs, the Enron scandal, proportional representation and the shame of belonging to a nation that produced both the Teletubbies and the Tweenies.

Sitting beside the lake, we watched a grebe diving and tried to guess where he would surface next, before splitting the newspaper between us to read as we munched bacon sandwiches.

A detour to the shops, and we reached home as the schools turned out. No sooner were we indoors than the doorbell began its late afternoon racket as younger son's friends began to show up. Disgusted by the noise and cavortings up and down the stairs, older son grabbed his jacket and headed off to find company more interesting to a 13-year-old.

Later, we pitched in together to cook dinner, sort out washing and scratch the surface of the serious housework this place of ours needs. Maybe one day we'll wake up to find the cleaning fairy has visited in the night? Younger son worked out how to turn his Lego car into a four-wheel drive while his brother and I wrestled some German verbs to the ground; they played chess, we all played 'Spots and Arrows' – a Kafkaesque version of Snakes and Ladders in which nobody ever gets anywhere at all, and then, somehow, it was bedtime. Tomorrow may be pretty similar; there again, we might decide to hit town, mooch in the library, head off to an exhibition or take a train to look at Salisbury Cathedral. One of the boys may be on a poetry jag, or decide to research Hitler or the Australian outback. It's impossible to say until we get up.

You've seen what I mean by 'chaotic' by now, but out of all this seemingly random activity and drifting conversation, what I can see is two people with a huge range of knowledge, some pretty impressive specialist subjects, strong opinions and a vocabulary with which to express them. I don't know exactly how they have come to know so much about things I can sometimes barely understand, but, as they say, if it ain't broke, don't fix it. We'll just keep right on playing it by ear and, no doubt, my sons will carry on surprising me!

Terri Dowty, home-educating parent

Doing exams

One of the biggest concerns is about exams. However it is quite possible for home educated children to take GCSE's, A/S levels, A levels and GNVQ's if they want to. They can be taken at the same age as their peers who are at school or they can be taken at different times. A number of exams can be taken together or they can be taken individually, thereby reducing the stress and allowing the student to focus on a smaller number of subjects at a time. But there is no requirement for children to take exams and it is up to each family if and how they do it.

Exams can be approached in a number of ways. The different examination boards will provide syllabuses and past exam papers. Students can work towards exams with the help of their parents or a tutor if necessary, and can take them as an external candidate at an examination centre. Alternatively there are many different distance learning programmes available. Details of these are available from the home education organisations. Another option is for students to enrol at a local further education college. Some colleges are prepared to take students who are under the age of sixteen.

Many home-educated students have been extremely successful in examinations and there have been multiple cases of children taking various subjects a number of years in advance of their peers at school and receiving good grades. Little research has been done in this country in this field, but a recent American study found that home-educated children are on average two years ahead of their peers at school.

Another family's experience
We are about to become retired home educators. Yesterday we went to our local College of Further Education to arrange courses for Laurence (16 years) for the autumn term. He has never attended school. He has completed his education to GCSE standard but with the exception of English and Maths, he is not interested in taking the exams. He wants to do a City and Guilds IT course with an additional course in computer aided design and manufacture, and he can't wait to get started.

Laurence's sister, Helen (17 years) learnt at home with him until she was 15, and since September 1999 she has been studying piano and bassoon at a specialist music school 400 miles away from home. Although they have shared many experiences in their formative years their individual personalities, interests and learning styles could not be more different from each other.

We have always believed that their education began on the day that they were born and we have very happy memories of the learning experiences that filled the first few years of their lives. We played together, we read books, we visited lots of people, we went for walks, we went to the seaside, we grew vegetables and looked after animals and made food and washed up, we made things, we painted and drew and danced and sang and pretended . . . and we wondered and talked and told stories and looked at everything under the sun. Sometimes the two children were horrible to each other and the fur flew, but most of the time they liked each other's company. It would have been an act of violence to separate the two of them when Helen reached school age as they shared so much and enjoyed so many things together. We had also built up the weekly round of activities which they shared; toddler gym, a mother and toddler group, story time at the library and various other regular meetings with friends.

We had made the decision already anyway, as we saw very early on that Helen was learning rapidly through the countless questions that she asked every day. She learned to read early and she loved books of all kinds. Our days were filled with conversations, particularly as we did not have a television. School seemed to be a rather unnecessary disruption, and we knew that this remarkably effective way of learning could not continue in a busy primary classroom.

I must admit, though, that I did get nervous at one point and we went to visit the local nursery school when Helen was three. It was a bustling, efficient and welcoming class and places were greatly sought after. Laurence and I watched from the sidelines as Helen went around to the different groups of children, joining in briefly and then moving on. Then she spotted the 'big' children who were cutting and sticking pictures from a catalogue and writing the names of the things underneath. Here was something she liked to do! Imagine her disappointment when she was told by the kindly assistant that she was not old enough to join in as these children were going to school next term. Would she like to play with the sand and water instead? Helen's answer was a decided 'No!' and she couldn't understand why she wasn't allowed to take part. We didn't go back there again.

I can still remember the day on which Helen should have started school. For some reason we had an awful day; the two children screamed and thumped each other and broke things and misery prevailed. I felt completely unable to improve the situation and I did wonder how long home education would last at this rate. Fortunately it turned out to be a rather unlucky coincidence as everything was fine the following day. There have been difficult times as well as many good experiences over the years, but I have yet to meet a home educator who didn't admit that there were times when boarding school suddenly seemed a very attractive option.

At first we used to have 'school' for a while in the morning when I sat down with Helen and we did writing, counting and various workbooks and learning activities. Laurence used to clamour to join in and he resented being fobbed off with toys on the floor. Mayhem threatened as he insisted on being included, but he picked up a lot while I worked with Helen. Sometimes we didn't manage to do very much but we soon discovered that one-to-one learning was very intensive anyway, so progress was made. 'School' became one of their games, and it's interesting that Laurence learned to read without being formally taught. He must have learned a lot from listening to Helen, and I can remember her teaching him all the letters and their sounds when they were playing.

So our living and learning continued, and their education turned out to be fairly informal in the primary years. The concept of 'subjects' didn't seem relevant. The one area where we followed a scheme was in maths as it seemed important to cover the basics in an orderly fashion. Reading and writing became part of life for Helen but Laurence didn't like writing very much as he grew older. He developed into an active learner but he also learnt a massive amount from reading. We did science topics from time to time including weather projects, wildlife studies, chemistry topics, simple geology and physics experiments. We had fun studying science with other home educating friends as well.

Social life was always a priority for us, and we were one of the founding families of a local group which is still thriving today. We soon discovered that other families were as keen as we were to make a good social life for their children. We met in playgrounds and went to play in each other's houses; we got together for art, cooking, sport, music, singing, dancing, skating and many other activities. Later the group arranged lessons including skiing, swimming, athletics and other sports. We attended workshops run by museums and we went as a group to concerts and theatre trips. We joined a gamelan group, we arranged some philosophy workshops, French and German lessons were run by local families and we had many opportunities to learn together. For many years we had Christmas parties and a group visit to the local pantomime, when everyone squashed into our house for soup and baked potatoes beforehand. As well as taking part in our local home educators' club every Thursday we met regularly with the Bedfordshire folk, the North London group, the families in Cambridge and others as well. We had friends to stay and our children went to visit in return. Sometimes they would take work to do together with friends, and this was followed by much playing and pretending. In those days my car always seemed to be full to bursting with other people's children and the talk about computer games was endless.

All these varied activities involved learning to get on with other children – and their parents. Inevitably there were some fights and difficulties but these were learning experiences which were necessary, if somewhat painful at times.

I have worked in traveller education for years and Helen and Laurence also had the companionship of the gypsy children who came to our home every week for their education. We planned the work for the week ahead and I went over it with them when we met next time. Helen wanted to work in the same way, so she had her notebook as well. As time went on her organisational skills developed and she enjoyed academic work. She also discovered a passion for music, particularly the piano. Laurence's education evolved in a very different way. By nature intuitive and imaginative, he has become an active, hands-on learner who hates repetition and predictability. Last year he learned a lot from every aspect of making a pond in the back garden and his interest diverged into an exploration of wildlife and the natural world. At present his work centres upon his computer and he has taught himself a great deal by experimenting with all sorts of software. He learns with astonishing speed when he decides that he wants to find out about something, and we think that the methods of education that are used in school would not have suited his personality at all.

Helen decided to study for some GCSEs at home, preparing to take five subjects when she was 14. We sent for the syllabuses and bought the books and materials, and she studied mainly on her own with some invaluable help with French from two friends. Six months before the exams she surprised us by announcing that she wanted to audition for a place at a specialist music school. When she discovered that she would need a second instrument she threw herself into learning the bassoon, using an instrument of mine that had been gathering dust for years at home. Somehow she managed to continue with her GCSE work while she worked hard to reach a good standard on both piano and bassoon, and she achieved high grades in all her subjects. On the day of her last exam we heard that she had been offered a place at St Mary's Music School in Edinburgh. When we left her in the company of the other pupils for her first experience of school in September we shared her feelings of excitement and anticipation, and she confounded the sceptics by adjusting quickly and easily to the school environment.

People often ask us about our view of the benefits of home education for our family. Helen says that learning at home gave her the freedom to develop her interest in music without the negative effect of the pop culture which is so powerful in most schools. Laurence has had the time and the opportunity to devote his energies to computing, and it seems likely that his future will be in IT. For us the most important consideration is that it has enabled the children's personalities and abilities to develop naturally, without being forced to fit into the mould of school and the National Curriculum. They have been able to take charge of their own learning and they have made their own decisions about moving on from home education when they were ready to do so.

Jane Lowe, home-educating parent

Learning centres

There are a number of examples of groups of families working together to educate their children.

South East

Isle of Wight Learning Zone
c/o Pendowrie
Dennett Road
Bembridge
Isle of Wight
PO35 5XF
Tel: 01983 872490

Project established: 1999

Age range of children: All ages

Home educating cooperatively on the Isle of Wight

The Isle of Wight Learning Zone (IWLZ) is a group of about twenty-five home educating families offering support, resources and social contact. The group was started in July 1999 when a few home educators got together to discuss issues like dealing with the local education authority and the possible need for a small school. It started with six families. Whilst each family felt that they were coping well enough on their own they realised that children and adults alike might benefit from activities that brought in new people and new ideas. They also felt that there were other families in the area who might be unhappy with school to whom they could offer support, encouragement and inspiration.

Three ideas tied these families together as a group. First we felt that when we did something creative, broadly educational or just plain fun with our children, we could offer a few places to other children in the IWLZ. Second we wanted a newsletter that would publicise these activities and keep members in touch. Third we agreed to hold regular committee meetings in a child-friendly pub where we could meet new members and old and also draw up the beginnings of a constitution.

Within two months we had embarked on the first of many ambitious projects – a play which was written by the children and performed in public. Many new activities were organised including a sponsored walk and camp, a second play set in Georgian England, a midsummer camp by the sea, historical re-enactments and many workshops. The number of families involved in the group grew rapidly and has now stabilised at around twenty-five.

A core of committee members produce the newsletter, deal with publicity, the LEA, grants and new members. A coordinator keeps track of workshops and events. The principle of acceptance, inclusion and non-judgement underpins the group. In this environment many children have flourished, trying new things all the time, gaining friends, learning new skills. But the adults have gained as much, sharing interests and ideas and offering mutual support. There are sometimes disagreements and these are thrashed out allowing the group to move on. The IWLZ has proved itself to be a robust and optimistic group.

Rebecca Alexander, The Isle of Wight Learning Zone

The Otherwise Club
c/o 1 Croxley Road
London W9 3HH
Tel. 020 8969 0893
Email: info@choice in education.co.uk
Website: choice in education.co.uk

Project established: 1993

Age range of children: 0–18

Activities: Community centre for families who choose to educate their children out of school

A home education club in London

The Otherwise Club provides a regular meeting place and social space for families choosing to educate their children out of school. It has a small café and alternative education library.

Regular workshops are provided such as pottery, drama and a history group. Special events and group activities are also organised and these have included a visit from a mobile planetarium, puppet-making workshops, country dancing and visits from police dog handlers with their dogs. There are occasional educational outings to places such as The Theatre Museum and The Golden Hinde Ship. The Duke of Edinburgh Award scheme is run for older home-educated young people who have done a canoeing course and a skiing trip to France as part of their activities. The club produces a newsletter for home educators in Britain and abroad called *Choice in Education.*

Lesley Barson, The Otherwise Club

Midlands

The Learning Studio
5–7 Castle Green
Bishops Castle
Shropshire
SY9 5BY
Tel: 01588 630475
Website: www.livingvillage.com

Project established: 2000

Age range of children: 5–10

Activities: Projects include: music, gardening and hut building. Workshops include: drama, storytelling, crafts, games

A learning centre for home-educated children
The Learning Studio is a place for home-educated children to meet, play and work together. Parents participate but there is a facilitator who runs the studio most of the time. The children choose projects they want to work on and the facilitator and parents help them structure these ideas into projects which may last a few days or weeks.

Carole Salmon, The Learning Studio

For information

Choice in Education
PO Box 20284
London NW1 3WY
Website: www.choiceineducation.co.uk
Produces a newsletter and organises a summer home education festival.

Education Now/Centre for Personalised Education
113 Arundel Drive
Bramcote Hills

Nottingham
NG9 3FQ
Tel: 0115 925 7261
Website: Gn.apc.org/educationnow
Publishes books about home education and other educational alternatives.

Education Otherwise
PO Box 7420, London
N9 9SG
Tel: 0891 518303
Website: www.education-otherwise.org
Membership organisation offering support to home-educating families. Puts members in contact with others in their area.

Free Range Education
Website: www.free-range-education.co.uk
A website dedicated to providing information about educating at home. Includes an email advice service.

Herald
Kelda Cottage
Lydbrook
Glos
GL17 9SX
Tel: 01594 861107
Email: herald@altavista.net
Website: www.homeeducation.co.uk
Offers practical advice on designing individual schemes of work covering the eight main areas of the curriculum. Produces topic packs and other resources.

Home Education Advisory Service
PO Box 98
Welwyn Garden City
Herts
AL8 6AN
Tel/fax: 01707 371854
Email: enquiries@heas.org.uk
Website: www.heas.org.uk
Membership organisation offering support and producing resources. Produces a regular newsletter.

Islamic Home Schooling Advisory Network
P O Box 30671
London
E1 0TG
Tel/fax: 020 7790 9981
Email: ihsaneducation@hotmail.co
Provides information and support for Muslim parents who are home educating their children and raises awareness of other alternatives to mainstream education.

Schoolhouse
93 Blacklock Crescent
Linlathen
Dundee
DD4 8EE
Tel: 01382 646964
Fax: 01382 640472
Email: info@schoolhouse.org.uk
Website: www.schoolhouse.org.uk
Offers support and a regular newsletter to home educators in Scotland.

WES Homeschool
Balgrave House
17 Balgrave Street
Reading
Berkshire
RG1 1QA
Tel: 0118 958 9993
Provides structured work plans and tutorial support for home-educated children. Set up to support families living abroad but also works with families in the UK.

Distance learning

Civil Service Correspondence School
14 Baldock Street
Ware
Herts
SG12 9DZ
Tel: 01920 465926

International Correspondence School
8 Elliot Place
Clydeway Centre
Glasgow
G3 8EP
Tel: 0500 303333

National Extension College
The Michael Young Centre
Purbeck Road
Cambridge CB2 2HN
Tel: 01223 400350
Fax: 01223 400325
Email: info@nec.ac.uk
Website: www.nec.ac.uk
Offers over 140 courses for home study

GCSE's through the National Extension College – one family's experience

Our children took their GCSE's through the National Extension College (NEC) in Cambridge, and we found this a very straightforward way of sitting exams for those who are outside the mainstream system.

With NEC courses each student is allocated to a personal tutor who marks all their assignments, validates coursework and generally offers help by, for example, marking past exam papers. The NEC provides all the learning materials and tutorial support but the candidate is responsible for finding a nearby examination centre which takes external candidates. In our case this was a local school.

NEC courses cost around £225 for each GCSE subject and this can be paid by instalments. You can enrol by post, fax, phone or email at any time of year and there is no upper or lower age limit. Assignments are posted to the tutor who marks and returns them with comments. Most tutors are happy to be phoned or emailed if problems arise. The tutors have extensive knowledge of the requirements of the different exam boards, which can prove very useful. Students can take as long or short a time as they wish preparing for exams and can choose how many to take at one time.

Heather McCombie, home-educating parent

Oxford Open Learning
4 King's Meadow
Oxford
OX2 0DP
Tel: 01865 798022

Satellite School
18 Victoria Park Square
Bethnal Green
London
E2 9PF
Tel: 0208 983 1866
Fax: 0208 980 3447
Email: satelliteschool@aol.com
Provides educational services to children aged 5–16 who are unable to attend conventional school: typically this is due to ill health although students may also, for example, be abroad for extended periods or wish to prepare for additional examinations in subjects which are not available in their mainstream schools. Pupils follow an agreed study timetable devised for each student by specialist tutors. Daily lessons are received by email.

Further reading

Adcock, J. (1994) *In Place of School*, London: New Educational Press.

Dowty, T. (ed.), (2000) *Free Range Education*, Hawthorn Press: Stroud.

Hern, M. (ed.), (1995) *Deschooling our Lives*, British Columbia: New Society.

Holt, J. (1991) *How Children Learn*, London: Penguin.

Llewellyn, G. (1997) *The Teenage Liberation Handbook: How to Quit School and get a Life and Education*, Shaftesbury: Element Books.

Lowe, J. and Thomas, A. (2002) *Educating Your Child at Home*, London: Continuum.

Meighan, R. (ed.) (1992) *Learning from Home-based Education*, Nottingham: Education Now.

Meighan, R. (1997) *The Next Learning System*, Nottingham: Educational Heretics Press.

Meighan, R. (2001) *Natural Learning and the Natural Curriculum*, Nottingham: Educational Heretics Press.

Meighan, R. (2001) *Learning Unlimited*, Nottingham: Educational Heretics Press.

Rose, M. A. and Stanbrook, P. (2000) *Getting Started in Home Education*, Nottingham: Education Now.

Thomas, A. (1998) *Educating Children at Home*, London: Continuum.

Chapter 9

Flexible schooling

> Instead of a National Curriculum for education what is really needed is an individual curriculum for every child, within common guidelines maybe, but given expression in a formal contract between the home and the school.
>
> Charles Handy

For many children, going to school five days a week, six hours a day is too much. It can be noisy and intimidating. It can be tiring and stressful. And it can cramp their style. There are many different ways of learning and it is difficult for a teacher of a class of thirty or thereabouts to accommodate the different learning styles of all the pupils. This can leave some children not doing particularly well and feeling frustrated.

For some parents also it is too much. They want to be involved in their children's education but find it difficult to work with the school within the current school structure. Teachers have little time to communicate with parents about their child and this can leave parents feeling excluded. Moreover, come the end of the day or the end of the week, the child often feels she has done enough learning and is ready for a break, making it more difficult for parents to play a part in the education process. With the emphasis on academic standards and the introduction of literacy and numeracy hours a growing number of parents feel that education, particularly at primary age, is based too much in the classroom, leaving too little time for drama, music, sport, outdoor activities, project work and trips away from school. They want to find a way to strengthen these important aspects of learning and to enable their children to go to school, but not all day, every day. In short, they want a halfway house and the flexibility to adapt the system to the needs of their own child – part-time school, part-time home education.

It *is* possible and in recent years the phenomenon of flexitime schooling has been established. Parents can make an agreement with the school to share responsibility for their child's education, sending her to school for some of the time and educating her at home for the remainder. This can take a number of different forms, for example sending the child to school for particular lessons which are perceived as difficult to do at home – drama, science or sport for instance, or perhaps splitting the week so that three days are spent at school followed by two days at home. Alternatively children can do blocks of time at school, followed by blocks at home and the blocks can be anything from a week, to a term or even a whole year, so that the child has a year at home followed by a year at school.

The option of flexitime schooling appears to have been taken up most often for children of primary age. The transition from nursery education to primary school is huge and for many children, full-time schooling at the age of four is too much. In a number of European countries children do not start full-time education until the age of six or seven and some parents here in the UK, questioning the wisdom of committing their four year-olds to full-time school, have pressed schools to allow their children to continue on a part-time basis until they are ready to attend full time. In other cases parents who have witnessed the negative impact – in the form of over-tiredness, boredom, withdrawal or irritability – of full-time school on their child, have come to an agreement with the school to withdraw the child for part of the week. Some flexitime arrangements have been instigated by families of children with special educational needs. They have been desperate because the child's school has been unable to provide the specialist help which the child needs and have arranged for the child to be absent from school on a regular basis to have tuition with an outside expert, for instance a dyslexia specialist. Other such arrangements have been made by families not wanting to launch into full-time home schooling but who, nevertheless, would like to play a more active part in their child's education.

The key factors are the flexibility of the family, the ability to respond to the needs of the child and the cooperation of the school. As far as flexibility is concerned, this is seen as an ideal option for some parents, enabling them to work part time but also to play an active part in their child's learning. For most however it is an impossibility because of the demands of earning a living.

The biggest hurdle is the attitude of the school and the local education authority. Whilst some parents have been successful in reaching a mutually acceptable agreement with their child's school, others have met with opposition and in some cases hostility to the idea. Schools can see such an arrangement as disruptive, not only for the child in question but for others in the class who do not have this option. But these difficulties are not insurmountable, and some families who have been keen on the idea of flexitime schooling have managed to persuade their local school that it would be workable and also in the best interests of their child.

How to go about it

Parents wishing to set up a flexitime schooling arrangement must approach the school, setting out their reasons. It is up to the head teacher and the governing body whether or not to agree to the request. The school may well approach the local education authority for advice but ultimately the decision rests with the school.

It is essential for parents to have the agreement of the school so that the child's absence is recorded as authorised leave. Without this the local education authority can take action against parents for keeping their child away from school.

It is in the interests of both the school and the family to draw up a written agreement so that each side knows what to expect of the other. Such an agreement could include details of when the child will attend; information about school records, reports and parent/teacher consultations; clarification of the statutory rights of parents and details about how to terminate the agreement.

Under such an agreement the child is registered at the school and the school receives full funding for the child from the LEA. The child, as a pupil at a state-funded school, is subject to the National Curriculum. The LEA Inspector may wish to visit the home to check up on the education the child is receiving when not at school, and this will be judged in terms of the National Curriculum. This is different from inspections of home educating families who are not subject to the National Curriculum. Parents need not be unduly concerned by this however, as their child is likely to fulfil many of the National Curriculum targets while at school and it is probable that the work done at home will encompass others, though perhaps in a less structured way than at school.

Parents of flexitime children may well consider that their child is doing enough National Curriculum related work at school and use time away from school to take a completely different approach, perhaps following the child's own interests with specific projects or adopting a more active and practical approach. Other parents may wish to use this time to reinforce and extend learning that has taken place at school with the aim of improving the child's academic attainment, either by giving the child individual attention or by using the services of a tutor.

The legal situation

Flexitime schooling is completely legal. As David Deutsch and Kolya Wolf explain in their book *Home Education and the Law* (1991):

> For some parents the ideal is to educate their children at home for part of the time, and have them attend school for the remainder. This is sometimes called 'flexi-schooling'. Combining schooling and non-schooling education in any proportions is perfectly legal, provided that the net effect is to provide proper education for the child (and the LEA must satisfy itself that this is so). However the school in question must agree to the arrangement. In a flexi-schooling arrangement the child is a registered pupil at the school and is deemed to be 'absent with leave' under sections 39(2) and 39(5) of the Education Act 1944 during periods when he is being educated away from the school.

The 1944 Education Act has now been superseded by the 1996 Act, the relevant section of which states that 'the child shall not be taken to have failed to attend regularly at the school by reason of his absence from the school (a) with leave' – Section 444(3).

According to section 444(9) leave can be granted 'by any person authorised to do so by the governing body or proprietor of the school'.

What is clear is that whereas parents have a right to full time education for their child and they have the right to home educate their child if they so wish, there is no automatic right to flexitime schooling. The decision rests with the school, and the head teacher or governing body are fully entitled to turn down a request for such an arrangement if they so wish.

Advantages and disadvantages

As with all things there are advantages and disadvantages – for the child, for the parents and for the school. For the child, the benefits include a more varied and personalised education and the option to choose how much time to spend at school and at home. For children who find school stressful this can be a huge relief and can make the difference between hating school and liking it or even between attending regularly (albeit for a shorter week) and not attending at all. The child can have greater input into decisions about their learning when not at school and can learn in a range of different ways and different places – indoors and outdoors – and from different people. The main disadvantage is the lack of continuity at school in terms of school work and also with friends.

As far as parents are concerned, the main advantages include greater involvement in their child's education and the possibility of a closer relationship due to increased contact (though this can work both ways). There are the accompanying difficulties of integrating this role with any work that they do and the increased demands on their time. There is also the challenge of keeping in touch with the school and nego- tiating a workable relationship with the child's teacher. The arrangement works best where there is good communication between the parents and the teacher so that each knows what the other is doing.

For the teachers there are also pros and cons. It is easier to teach a child who is at school out of choice rather than compunction and is therefore likely to be more motivated. And one less child in the class even for part of the week releases a little time for the other pupils. On the other hand, extra time is needed to liaise with the parents. Dealing with a child who has missed significant chunks of class work also creates extra work.

Whilst the majority of parents who have set up flexitime schooling with their child's school have been happy with the arrangement, there have been cases where it has not worked. There have been examples where the school, with or without pressure from the LEA, has changed its mind after such an arrangement has been made and has withdrawn the facility. Some head teachers, after giving it a try, have decided that it just does not work in their situation.

Examples

There are many examples of a more flexible approach to education in America. Positive encouragement for innovation in a number of states has led some schools to offer a more personalised approach to learning in which a curriculum and timetable is negotiated for each child, and this may involve periods of home study. In California, the Independent Study Program allows for children to study part time at school and part time at home. Funding is shared between the two. There are cyber or virtual schools which children can attend from home. In Alberta in Canada, families who sign up for home-based education can rent a computer from the school district and access online lessons and support from teachers. This programme is linked directly to ten schools in the province. In Elk Island District students meet their teachers fortnightly for presentations and tutorials whilst the bulk of their work is carried out at home. In Australia too, the possibility of partnerships between state schools and home-based learners is being investigated. This is particularly valuable in cases where the family lives a long way from the school.

In the UK some primary and secondary schools within the state sector as well as some small, alternative schools have agreed to flexitime schooling arrangements. A rather different model is the Satellite School in London, which supports children who are learning at home through online tutorials or by phone or fax. A further option for a particularly able child is registration full time or part time on a college or university course where the child has reached the required standard.

In this country any special arrangements have to be funded by the family. As yet there is no financial support for families who choose such an option.

The future

Flexitime schooling has only come into being in the last ten years and to date less than one hundred families have been successful in making such an arrangement with their local school. This is a very small number, but is it likely to increase? There are three reasons why it might.

First, the government, rightly, has placed much emphasis on parental involvement in their children's education. It has long been known – and research bears this out – that the children of parents who take an interest in their education do better and yet the structure of schools makes it difficult for parents to be involved. Teachers are so stretched that, on the whole, they can give little time to parents above the cursory parent/teacher consultations which take place two or three times each year. The five or ten minutes generally allotted to each family is hardly enough for parents and teachers to engage in a real dialogue about the child's learning. Parents who try to find out more about what is happening in their child's class to enable them to offer support at home are not always welcomed. The main role that interested parents currently play at school, apart from as a governor, is as a fund-raiser on the parent teacher association, and this is a wasted opportunity. To an extent flexitime schooling forces the issue by drawing teachers and parents together in a dialogue. It gives schools a way of engaging with parents to support their child's learning.

Second, with the increasing use of computers in education, children do not need to be at school all the time. Some of their work could be done as individual study at home. This is likely to be more effective if parents are involved and know what the work consists of. With the rise in the number of home computers and the growing use of email, communication with parents need not be arduous. If schools were to make use of new technology in this way and encourage some home study it could free up teachers and resources significantly.

Third, the structure of schools has to change. New structures and new ways of learning are required to meet the demands of a fast-changing world. There are many pressures on the current system and the cracks are showing. A more flexible approach to education is needed and flexitime schooling offers one bridge to a new and better way.

Flexitime schooling: one family's experience

After thirteen years of flexitime schooling my two children started school full time last September. It was the end of a privileged era with the best of both worlds. 'You are brave teaching them at home,' was the stock reaction. But that's not what I did. We went to work/school for three days a week and had a four-day weekend – just doing more of what other people do at weekends. And fortunately, the children proved – to the LEA inspector as well as to the world at large – that they were learning most of the time, or at least consolidating their learning. They cooked and washed up, gardened and shopped. They cycled and bladed, danced and sang. We stayed in bed reading and listening to the radio or leaped up and went off on the train for long weekends to places further afield than two days allow. They learned to skate on empty rinks and to swim in spacious pools. Librarians had time to help them, adults all over the place had time to engage with them, and younger children lapped up their attention as skills were passed down seamlessly. We did not 'do' rocket science – my main vicarious ambitions were that they could work the world adequately and keep themselves happy. A side effect is that they are both good at communicating, in all sorts of media and with all sorts of people.

Each term they had the choice to go full time. Bea took up the offer for half a term, and then reverted to three days. Knowing that the school week was only three days meant that Felix could contain his very high energy and insistent curiosity, and Bea could conserve her post-glandular fever low energy. At school, concepts are explained several times in the course of a fortnight, so they knew that if there were things that they had not picked up in one week, they would be covered again the next week for all those who had not understood first time round or who were off ill. They must have missed some things, but it never appeared to worry them.

Bea answered questions at the Human Scale Education Alternatives in Education Fair in 2001. 'Didn't you have problems maintaining friendships?' 'No, not at all because we could always meet up after school on the days I was not there.' 'Didn't you find it hard to keep up with the work?' 'No, because I had picked a lot of it up in other ways at home, and I got the chance to do lots of things that I wouldn't otherwise have had time to.' 'Didn't it mean that everyone in your class wanted to do it?' 'No, some of them hadn't even noticed I was not there for two days a week until Year six. My friends sometimes wished they could do it too but most parents don't seem to want to spend more time with their children. They are glad when the holidays end.' 'Would you do the same with your children?' 'Yes definitely, I really recommend it. I made friends at school and did a few interesting things, but then I could be with my family, the younger children in the street and adult friends, and learn the things I was interested in the rest of the time.'

All those years ago I had been delighted when the Chief Education Officer, the head teacher and the Governors had agreed that we could try it out. Only much later, when I had been contacted by hundreds of parents who were struggling to get a part-time agreement with their child's school, did I realise just how privileged we were. We had not had to phone in sick two days a week for several years. We had not had to move house to get what we wanted. We had not even had to justify ourselves to the two inspectors who left the house wishing that more children had the same opportunity. Both children graduated from primary to secondary school with grades above average – despite their mother having given up project work at home with them after the second attempt (one child was happy measuring tree trunks for ages while the other was soon bored having climbed them). We never even tried to 'dovetail' with work at school or even follow the National Curriculum, and yet Felix and Bea were successfully measured by it at home when the inspectors called.

What did I learn meanwhile? I learned that children learn all the time unless they are prevented; that they are most at ease pacing themselves and choosing when they leave home; that the world, whether a kitchen or a bus garage, is the most efficient learning resource available with very little effort needed on the part of the parent facilitator, and that if you expect them to be enthusiastic and responsible, for the most part they are – as long as I am cheerful too. So why didn't we home school? Because I enjoy my work outside the house, because I wanted the variety for them and for me, because there wasn't anyone else who wanted to home educate in our local community, and I did not want to do it without a community context. Why didn't we just go to school full time? Because it seems odd to post small children into a room with twenty-eight other children and one adult for five days a week. Let's hope that in the twenty-first century we realise that learning comes in all shapes and sizes and have the courage to *flex* and *let flex* accordingly.

Kate Oliver

Further reading

Deutsch, D. and Wolf, K. (1991) *Home Education and the Law*, Oxford: Deutsch and Wolf.

Meighan, R. (1988) *Flexi-schooling*, Nottingham: Education Now Books.

Oliver, K. (ed.) (1999) *Flexi-time schooling*, Bath: Human Scale Education or on the web at www.warwick–district.org.uk/flexi

Part 3

Alternative approaches in the state system

Chapter 10

State schools

Alternative ways of working

> The only real object of education is to leave a man in the condition
> of continually asking questions.
>
> Tolstoy

State schools, by definition, are not alternative as they are part of the
state apparatus and exist, at least in part, to prepare children to join
the work force and contribute to the economy. The introduction,
over the past two decades, of market values into the state education
system – as expressed in SATs, league tables and competition between
schools – threaten the essence of what education should be about,
namely the development of the individual child. As a consequence
growing numbers of young people are being sidelined by a system
which does not respond to their needs.

This situation is being exacerbated by the creeping privatisation of
schools. Private companies are being encouraged to take over failing
schools and local education authorities with the remit of turning them
around. But business will only be interested if there is profit to be made
and this can only be achieved at the expense of children, for example
by cutting provision, or reducing the number of teachers. There is no
evidence to suggest that schools run by business achieve higher standards.

Furthermore the education process itself is being commercialised.
Over 85 per cent of schools are now involved in some sort of
commercial activity. Vouchers and tokens from a wide range of products
are funding books, sports equipment and computers and many
companies are producing teaching resources which are free to schools
but which promote the companies' products. Such activities are rapidly
turning our schools into marketing vehicles and children into compliant
consumers.

To counter such damaging trends a number of state schools are trying to find ways of working with children that encapsulate alternative principles, and some interesting projects are taking place across the country. There are no simple answers, and each school has to respond to its own unique situation with the staff and resources that are available and within the constraints laid down by government. Different schools across the country present very different challenges and consequently the range of projects is diverse.

This chapter looks at projects which, in some way, address the key issues outlined in Chapter 1 of making schools more equitable, more inclusive or more environmentally sustainable. The projects are divided into broad categories which relate closely to the elements considered by the charity Human Scale Education to be essential constituents of education (as discussed in Chapter 2):

- Positive relationships
- A holistic approach to learning
- Democratic participation
- Partnership with parents and the local community
- Environmental sustainability
- Smaller structures.

Positive relationships

All schools know that positive relationships amongst pupils, between pupils and staff, amongst staff, with parents and with the local community are vitally important. But achieving them, especially in large schools, is a significant challenge. It involves finding ways to create an atmosphere of openness and trust in which all people can feel valued. Many projects addressing this aspect of school life have been instigated.

At Ralph Allen School in Bath there is a mentoring programme whereby new students in Year 7 have a mentor in Year 10, someone with whom they can discuss any issues or difficulties arising from their transfer from primary school. This system helps with integration into secondary school and has the added benefit of encouraging friendships across the year groups.

Teachers and pupils at Stantonbury Campus in Milton Keynes are on first name terms and this creates an atmosphere of informality which is popular with students and contributes to more open and positive relationships.

Peer mediation is increasingly used in schools as a way of dealing with difficulties. In a number of schools students are trained as counsellors and can be called upon to help defuse conflict situations within the school. Successful schemes are in operation at Highbury Fields School in Islington and Acland Burghley school in Camden.

A similar scheme has been introduced at Dog Kennel Hill Primary School in Southwark, where Year 6 children are trained to be 'helpers'. At break and lunch times they actively look out for problem situations or for fellow students who are unhappy. They know which kinds of situations they cannot deal with and call upon teachers as appropriate.

Circle time is commonly used in primary schools as a way of enabling children to express their thoughts and feelings and to solve problems in the class. There are strict ground rules – only one person at a time can speak while others listen. The circle provides a safe environment for exploration of ideas and can help to raise children's self-esteem and group acceptance. Jack Lobley Primary School in Essex has used the circle time approach to improve behaviour at the school.

The importance of dialogue in establishing and maintaining relation-ships is recognised and can be used by teachers in all areas of the curriculum in collaborative group work. By carefully mixing groups teachers can use this as a tool to enhance racial and religious tolerance. In addition to the benefits to relationships it has the advantage of helping students deepen their understanding of the subject.

Emotional literacy is increasingly recognised as a key factor in effective learning. When people are aware of their own emotions they can be more open with others and are also more open to learning. A number of schools are now working to create an environment in which children feel emotionally secure. Cavendish First School in Yorkshire is one such school. An ongoing project involving working with artists has produced a totem pole of feelings and a collective poem which has been turned into an animation entitled *Inside Me*. The school is taking the project further by building a special room where children can go when they need some space. It is a place where they can think, talk, draw and be peaceful away from the hurly burly of school life.

A holistic approach to learning

The National Curriculum inhibits the ability of schools to offer a holistic and integrated approach to education because it divides learning into subject areas. In secondary education particularly, and increasingly in primary schools, cross-curricular work is rare. There is provision within education legislation for schools to apply to the Secretary of State for Education for exemption from all or parts of the National Curriculum but surprisingly, few schools have taken advantage of this opportunity. Very many schools are concerned however by the focus on academic achievement alone and are looking for ways to develop the whole child.

Some schools have introduced an alternative curriculum for disaffected students in Years 10 and 11 and this has generally been successful. Harriet Costello School in Basingstoke has disapplied the National Curriculum for students that it deemed were 'on the edge of school life' and in its place students have followed more vocational courses as well as attending sessions at the local college. Some of the students involved in this scheme acknowledge that it saved them from exclusion.

Cramlington Community High School in Northumberland has instituted an annual Investigations Week. During this week the timetable is abandoned and students pursue projects in small groups using their teachers as mentors. The idea for this special week arose from the head teacher's belief that there is too great an emphasis on *what* children learn and that more attention should be paid to *how* they learn. In the first such Investigations Week there was an impressive array of cross-curricular projects including presenting a play about global dangers, building a biodome, producing an alternative energy model for the school and creating a community art feature. Students worked hard and were impressed by their achievements. The only pity is that such a worthwhile innovation is restricted to one week of the year, when these were probably some of the most valuable learning experiences the children will have had during their school career.

A number of schools in the Merseyside area and elsewhere have been working with Howard Gardner's theory of multiple intelligences. This theory holds that there are a number of distinct forms of intelligence and that people are intelligent in different ways. The logical/mathematical intelligence called upon predominantly at school is only one kind of intelligence. The other intelligences include linguistic, spatial, bodily kinaesthetic, musical, interpersonal and intrapersonal and more recently it has been suggested that an eighth – ecological intelligence – should be added. These schools have been finding ways of engaging all the intelligences by encouraging different approaches to learning. In this way, all children can succeed – not just those who have logical/mathematical intelligence.

Democratic participation

It is important that students are involved in decision-making so that they feel as though they have a stake in their school and also learn about democracy. There is a range of ways in which schools can encourage student participation and the most well known of these is to establish a school council. Many schools, at secondary level in particular, have done this. It is important that students believe that their councils make a real contribution to school decision-making, otherwise they are not taken seriously. In too many schools students think that their councils are not allowed to discuss any issues of importance and also see decisions they have made being overruled by senior management. This is worse than not having a council at all, as it gives students the message that their views do not count.

The school student council at Cotham School in Bristol is taken very seriously indeed. It has the wholehearted support of the head teacher and time is made in the timetable for it to meet on a regular basis. The council has its own budget and has made decisions about the running of the school which are visible to all students. One example of this is the awarding of the contract for the school catering service, a

Figure 10.1 A school student council meeting at Cotham School.
Credit: Jane Thomas

decision which was made after much consultation and research by the student council.

One problem in large schools is that the majority of children feel removed from the workings of the council. At Cotham mechanisms are in place by way of smaller year group sessions to ensure that all students have the chance to have their views represented at full council meetings and to receive feedback which can then be discussed.

Increasing student democracy is not just about the running of the school, but also concerns student input into decisions about learning and assessment. At Sharnbrook School in Bedford students are involved in discussions about what they are learning, how they are assessed and also the quality of the teaching. The project at Sharnbrook, called *Students as Researchers*, has been instrumental in bringing about real improvements at the school.

At Highfield Junior School in Plymouth primary children have been involved in decisions as diverse as buying furniture, staff appointments and behaviour policy. In one instance children wanted to deal with the persistent bad behaviour of a member of their class. After lengthy discussions they decided to invite the child's parents in to school to discuss the situation with them and look for solutions together. Over time this led to significant improvements. As far as staff appointments are concerned, the school has found that when children are involved in choosing teachers they have a personal commitment to working positively with the new member of staff.

James Gillespie School in Edinburgh has used a democratic process to try to bring about whole school change. By working in the first instance with one tutor group, each of the different groups associated with this tutor group, namely students, parents, teachers and senior management, met individually to discuss their experiences of school and obstacles to learning. After a series of meetings in which a wide range of issues was explored these different groups came together to hear each other's viewpoints and discuss ways of improving the school. This was the beginning of a lengthy process of change but offers a model of how such a process can be initiated.

Partnership with parents and the local community

Schools have an important part to play in community regeneration. Projects involving parents and the local community benefit both the school and the community itself. It is a question of encouraging people from the community to come into the school and also of taking the children out into the community for different projects. When the community is used as a resource for the children it has the effect of bringing learning to life because it relates what they are studying to their life outside school. When the school is used as a resource for the community it raises the profile of the school locally and strengthens local support.

Maximising the relationship between the school and the local community is particularly important to small, rural primary schools which may be under threat of closure. Already local people may see the school as the heart of the community, but unless it is used as a facility for all it may be deemed expendable by the local council on grounds of cost. Lowick Primary School in Cumbria is responding to this challenge by developing the school as a multimedia resource for the community.

The head teacher at West Walker Primary School in Newcastle felt that it was very difficult to raise the attainment of her pupils because learning was not valued in the community beyond school. With high unemployment parents found it hard to see the point of education. In response to this situation she worked hard to draw parents into the life of the school involving them in discussions and setting up new initiatives. A community centre with multi-agency input and adult education facilities was established on the school site. Mentoring schemes with local firms were set up so that children could gain first-hand experience of a working environment. A social services family worker was employed. Parents, teachers and children worked together with architects to design a play park. School-based projects such as a breakfast club and partnership schemes to help children with time keeping and homework were also instigated. All these initiatives are working together to transform the neighbourhood.

St Paul's Community School in Birmingham is also part of a wider community regeneration project. It belongs to a neighbourhood forum which includes a Welfare to Work programme as well as a number of environmental projects and family welfare schemes. The school works closely with a range of agencies and local authority departments and is setting up a permanent body where mutual problems can be discussed, community solutions discovered and implementation initiated.

Babington Community Technology College in Leicester set up an early years education partnership to provide support to disadvantaged parents in the area, to help them improve the prospects of their children before they start school. The project works in conjunction with local primary schools and has established an informal discussion and support group for parents of babies and young children, a parents' and children's group with different activities for 1–3 year-olds and a series of modules for parents of 3–5 year-olds to discuss issues such as learning through play and behaviour management. It has been highly successful in raising the confidence of parents with respect to parenting and has therefore impacted positively on parents, their children and participating schools. In 2001 this work was taken over by SureStart. New facilities have been built in the local area to promote this work in the future.

Ilfracombe College in Devon has, over the years, implemented a number of schemes to address the question of social and economic regeneration and to enhance the life experiences of its young people. Working with a range of partners it established a National Youth Arts Festival which draws young people from all over the UK, and this has acted as a stimulus for local young people. It has also initiated an annual Ilfracombe Victorian Celebration which has had the effect of encouraging local people to celebrate local heritage whilst at the same time creating a major tourist attraction. The school has been instrumental in the establishment of a youth and community centre and has also helped to set up a music centre which is used by local musicians for rehearsing and recording. The pupil referral unit is based at the youth and community centre and from here young people who are disaffected with school are involved in a wide range of regeneration projects in the community.

Little London Community Primary School, an inner-city school in Leeds has established an extensive programme of in-school and after-school activities for parents as well as children. Crèche facilities are provided while parents attend courses. As parents' confidence has flourished more and more courses and activities have been added. This has had the effect of establishing a culture of learning at the school, as children benefit from seeing their parents as learners too. It has also contributed to creating strong relationships between teachers, parents and staff, who meet in a range of circumstances. The parents now run a breakfast club at the school and the school is also used as a venue by local organisations for a wide range of activities for children and adults. This work has had a huge effect in improving the ethos of the school and the attainment of the children.

Environmental sustainability

A mountain of evidence indicates the damage that humans are wreaking on the planet and there is growing recognition that we need to find ways of living that are more environmentally sustainable. The Agenda

21 agreement made at the Rio Earth Summit in 1992 sought to involve young people and schools in the transition to a more environmentally sustainable society, but developments in this area have been slow. It was recognised that schools could make a vital contribution by placing environmental issues at the heart of their policies and practices. Some schools are beginning to take this challenge seriously but many more must follow suit so that young people understand the connection between their own behaviour and global issues.

Ansford Community School in Somerset is working to integrate environmental issues across the curriculum. They have produced an education for sustainability policy which outlines the knowledge and understanding, skills, values and attitudes that students wish to gain. Their first cross-curricular project was to create a herb garden and this involved the history, food, English, science, technology and art departments. Since then there has been an environment week comprising a range of environmental activities, an environment day involving children from local primary schools and a school production on the theme of looking after the planet, called *Trash*. This was written and performed by students. Staff training sessions are a vital part of this project and have helped staff incorporate environmental issues into their subjects, as well as challenging their lifestyles. The school has an environmental working party comprising students, teachers and governors which oversees the whole project.

Royton and Crompton Comprehensive School in Oldham has implemented an education for sustainability curriculum as a means of enhancing the curriculum as a whole. This is part of a drive to broaden students' horizons so that they understand their responsibilities as global citizens. Students are encouraged to explore their own values and attitudes and develop their skills as active citizens in the local and global communities. The school is creating a spiral curriculum so that cross-curricular themes relating to education for sustainability are incorporated across the curriculum and revisited according to the students' stage of development.

A large number of schools, both primary and secondary, are developing their school grounds to grow food, encourage a range of wildlife, rear animals and give pupils a chance to connect with the natural world. The charity, Learning through Landscapes, has been instrumental in supporting schools in finding ways of using their land productively as well as creating a valuable resource for learning.

Weobley School in Herefordshire has installed a special boiler which burns fuel made from willow which is produced in the local area.

Cassop Primary School in County Durham has installed a wind turbine which provides 90 per cent of the school's energy requirements.

Junk food and fizzy drinks have been banned from Wolsey Junior School in South London and children can buy fruit from the tuck shop instead. As 40 per cent of the children are on free school meals staff felt that it was essential that these children received plenty of fresh fruit and vegetables. The school has reported a significant improvement in behaviour and concentration, which it links to the reduction of additives in the children's diet.

The national cycle network, Sustrans, is assisting schools in implementing environmental transport policies whereby students are encouraged to walk or cycle to school. 'Walking buses', whereby children meet up on their school route and walk to school together, are supervised by adults and are a means of taking children to school collectively.

Smaller structures

The final and potentially most significant constituent of positive change is smaller structures. This is an area in which very little work has been done in the UK in spite of the wealth of research evidence and successful models in America. Some examples from America are discussed in Chapter 11.

Smaller structures are arguably the key to effective school transformation because they make it more possible for the other features outlined above to be brought into play. Within smaller schools and smaller classes the democratic participation of all those who are involved with the school becomes more feasible. Smaller schools facilitate a greater sense of community because members can all know each other as individuals rather than merely as faces or names. Curriculum innovation towards a more holistic approach to learning is made possible by a school environment in which teachers know their students well. The improved relationships generally found within smaller schools make it easier for parents and members of the local community to become involved. Finally, the principles of citizenship and environmental sustainability can more easily be integrated by schools which are committed to cooperative and participative approaches to learning. Such methods are more readily employed by teachers working with smaller groups. These are just some of the advantages of smaller structures. Several examples of how schools have incorporated smaller structures are given below.

Stantonbury Campus in Milton Keynes has been run as a federation of smaller schools on one site since the 1980s. Each mini school or hall has its own distinctive atmosphere and its own head. Children attend one of the schools and stay within that school, with the same teachers and students and predominantly in the same building until they have done their GCSE's. By working in this way students have all the advantages of being part of a smaller school community whilst benefiting from the extensive resources of a large institution.

Seaford Head Community College in East Sussex is based on two sites – one for Key Stage 3 students and the other for Key Stages 4 and 5. Each site has around 700 students. The College is reculturing the Key Stage 3 site to create three separate Learning Communities within one school. Each Learning Community (of around 230 students) is again divided into three learning groups (of approximately 27 students in each group) in each of Years 7, 8 and 9. These three groups constitute a teaching team of 80–90 students with the same team of teachers who meet regularly to discuss learning and teaching. Staff believe that within these smaller Learning Communities greater emphasis can be placed on improving relationships, which is critical to raising attainment.

Nurture groups are small, special classes set up in some inner city primary schools for children who come from families which have difficulty in meeting their basic developmental needs. The aim of such groups is to lay the foundations for educational progress so that children are able to cope with mainstream schooling. These groups were first started in London in the 1970s, but their success with children from disadvantaged backgrounds has led to many more nurture groups being set up around the country.

The examples given in this chapter represent just some of the innovative projects which are being introduced around the country and many schools are working across several of these areas. The aim of giving these examples is to show a range of projects which are having a positive impact on the lives of students in state schools.

For information

Antidote
Fifth Floor
45 Beech Street
London EC2Y 8AD
Tel: 0207 588 5151

Fax: 0207 588 4900
Email: emotional.literacy@antidote.org.uk

Citizenship Foundation
Ferroners House
Shaftesbury Place
Aldersgate Street
London
EC2Y 8AA
Tel: 0207 367 0500
Website: www.citfou.org.uk

Community Education Development Centre
Unit C1 Grovelands Court
Grovelands Estate
Longford Road
Exhall
Coventry
CV7 9NE
Tel: 02476 588440
Fax: 02476 588441
Email: info@cedc.org.uk
Website: www.cedc.org.uk

Human Scale Education
Unit 8
Fairseat Farm
Chew Stoke
Bristol
BS40 8XF
Tel/fax: 01275 332516
Email: info@hse.org.uk
Website: www.hse.org.uk

Learning through Landscapes
Third Floor
Southside Offices
The Law Courts
Winchester
SO23 9DL
Tel: 01962 846258
Website: www.ltl.org.uk

National Foundation for Educational Research
The Mere
Upton Park
Slough
SL1 2DQ
Tel: 01753 747218
Website: www.nfer.ac.uk

Organic Network for Schools
Ryton Organic Gardens
Coventry
CV8 3LG
Tel: 02476 303517
Website: www.organic_schools.net

Schools Council UK
57 Etchingham Park Road
London
N3 2EB
Tel: 0208 349 2459
Website: www.schoolcouncils.org.uk

Sustrans
35 King Street
Bristol
BS1 4DZ
Tel: 0117 926 8893

Transforming Schools Network
37 Park Hall Road
East Finchley
London N2 9PT
Tel: 0208 365 3869
Email: transformingschools@seal.org.uk

WWF UK
Panda House
Weyside Park
Godalming
Surrey
GU7 1XR

Tel: 01483 426444
Website: www.wwf.learning.co.uk

Further reading

Apple, M. and Beane, J. (eds) (1999) *Democratic Schools: Lessons from the Chalkface*, Buckingham: Open University Press.
Bennathan, M. and Boxall, M. (1996) *Effective Intervention in Primary Schools: Nurture Groups*, London: David Fulton.
Craft, A. (1997) *Can you Teach Creativity*, Nottingham: Education Now.
Gardner, H. (1983) *Frames of Mind: The Theory of Multiple Intelligences*, New York: Basic Books.
Harber, C. (1995) *Developing Democratic Education*, Nottingham: Education Now.
Hicks, D. (2001) *Citizenship for the Future*, Godalming: WWF.
Rennie, J. (1999) *Branching Out: Schools as Community Regenerators*, Coventry: CEDC.
Sharp, P. (2001) *Nurturing Emotional Literacy: A Practical Guide for Teachers, Parents and those in the Caring Professions*, London: David Fulton.
Symons, G. (1998) *Making it Happen: Agenda 21 and Schools*, Godalming: WWF.
Titman, W. (1994) *Special Places, Special People*, Godalming: WWF/LTL.

Chapter 11

Small is beautiful

Lessons from America

> I cannot teach well a student whom I do not know.
>
> Professor Ted Sizer, *Horace's Hope*, 1996

There are many different kinds of schools and learning alternatives across America. Some are publicly funded, others are privately run and financed and some are a combination of the two.

The American *Almanac of Education Choices* lists the alternatives available in each state of which there are 49 for example in Alabama and 99 in Wisconsin whilst over 800 are listed for California. These include Steiner and Montessori schools, Amish schools, Carden Schools, Comer schools, free schools, holistic schools and many more individual initiatives such as the School for the Physical City, the School Without Walls, the School of the Future and the School within a School. In addition it is estimated that over two million American children are now educated at home.

A whole host of publicly funded alternatives have been established: of these magnet schools and charter schools are perhaps the most well known in the UK. Magnet schools (which were first started in the 1970s) are schools based on a specific theme or curricular focus and their aim, in many instances, has been to attract students from all sectors of a community to overcome problems of segregation. The charter school movement, a more recent initiative which began in the 1990s, was conceived to encourage educational innovation by freeing schools from state education laws. The state grants a charter or contract to a group of organisers – mostly groups of educators and parents – who design and run the school. These schools are public insofar as they cannot be selective or sectarian, cannot charge fees and are accountable for their results. They are funded on the same basis as normal state schools and are required to produce measurable gains in student achievement or else they must close. Well over 50 per cent of states have now passed charter legislation and more are considering the idea.

As the legislation differs from state to state, so too does the provision; but across the US there is a groundswell of desire for new approaches as increasing numbers of parents and teachers become concerned about the capacity of traditional schools to meet the needs of young people.

Events such as the shootings at Columbine High School in Colorado in 1999 have made many question the safety of huge high schools. Schools of 3–4,000 are not uncommon in America, and if these schools cannot vouch for the safety of their students parents are going to be less and less inclined to send their children. Whilst every parent wants their child to do well, even more important is the question of their physical safety and well-being.

The issue of school size is thus becoming a political concern in America. As it is a theme that has recurred throughout the book, this chapter will look at developments in publicly funded schools in which the issue of school size is addressed.

Research

An extensive body of research (compiled by the Small Schools Workshop based in Chicago) about the effectiveness of smaller schools has been amassed over the past 20 years. This research has found that in small schools:

- **Children** have better attendance rates and higher test scores
- They are more likely to participate in after-school activities and are less likely to be truants, gang members or substance abusers
- They feel more connected to and positive about their schools
- **Teachers** form closer bonds with students and with each other and are more committed to the school
- They also tend to be more innovative with the curriculum
- **Parents** are more involved with the school.

Furthermore the research indicates that small schools are more cost effective than large schools and that their benefits are more marked for children from disadvantaged backgrounds.

Whilst any such research is dismissed out of hand by the UK government which is fearful of the financial implications, it is driving policy in a growing number of American states. In Providence, the new schools superintendent has instructed all high schools to convert themselves into smaller, more personalised learning communities. In Chicago over 150 small high schools have been opened since 1990 and many more are in the pipeline. In the bay area of San Francisco parents have been so outraged by the quality of their local schools that they have precipitated major reforms in the area involving the creation of new small schools and the transformation of existing large schools into smaller learning communities. Other areas including Philadelphia, Washington State, Denver and Los Angeles are all moving in a similar direction. Radical reforms in New York have been underway for a number of years and have yielded significant improvements to the education system there.

It has to be stressed that it is not small schools per se that are important, because there can be bad small schools, but rather what smaller scale learning communities make possible in terms of teaching and learning. In America there is, as yet, no national curriculum so there is far greater freedom for teachers to use innovative approaches to teaching and learning – and this is the major factor underpinning the success of smaller schools.

Much of the work which is directed towards creating more personalised learning opportunities for students is being done in association with the Coalition for Essential Schools (CES). The Coalition is a school/university partnership that works across America to redesign American schools for better student learning and achievement. It was founded in 1985 by Professor Ted Sizer and is based on a set of principles which schools can sign up to and which are listed on the next page. Over 1000 schools have interacted with the Coalition since it was set up and it has become an important force for change in American education.

The Bill and Melinda Gates Foundation has been a major sponsor for many of these developments. Furthermore the federal government, through the US Department of Education, has recently announced a new initiative called the Small Learning Communities Program. This provides funds to encourage large schools to undertake the planning, implementation and expansion of small learning communities through research-based restructuring. Over $40 million has been allocated to this programme already and grants have been awarded to 350 schools across the US with a further 200 expected imminently.

> ## The common principles of the Coalition of Essential Schools
>
> Schools strive to:
>
> 1   Teach students to use their minds well
> 2   Emphasise depth of learning over breadth
> 3   Apply their goals to all students
> 4   Personalise teaching and learning
> 5   Embrace the metaphor 'student as worker' rather than teacher as 'deliverer'
> 6   Require students to demonstrate mastery through an 'exhibition' of their knowledge and skills
> 7   Stress a tone of decency and trust
> 8   Consider teachers as generalists committed to the entire school
> 9   Develop budgets that reflect CES priorities, for example by setting a student load of eighty pupils or less for each teacher
> 10   Model democratic and equitable practices.

Examples

A number of different models for reform based on small structures have emerged, and three of these models will be discussed below.

The small school model

Central Park East School

In recent years many new publicly-funded small schools have been established and it is increasingly recognised that where there is a need for new school places, particularly in urban areas, these are best provided within smaller schools. One well-established small school which has provided a model for many newer initiatives is the Central Park East Secondary School (CPESS) in East Harlem, New York.

CPESS was founded in 1985 and caters for around 450 students aged 13–18 (grades 7–12). About 90 per cent of the students are from ethnic minorities, 50 per cent receive free school meals and around 20 per cent are recognised as having special educational needs. Whilst the graduation rate from high school is around 55 per cent in traditional New York schools, CPESS graduates around 90 per cent of its students. A similar percentage of students proceed on to college.

Whilst the school is proud of these achievements its main aims are to ensure that students learn to use their minds well, that they become passionate about their work, they feel cared for and they learn to care for others. Much emphasis is placed on creating a community and fostering a sense of responsibility. The school is divided into houses of eighty and students remain in their house, with the same four or five teachers for two years. Each student has an individual advisor who can offer personal as well as academic support and regular time is made for advisory sessions.

In order to encourage students to use their minds well five key questions underpin the work in every subject and every lesson. Students are encouraged to consider what they are reading or hearing in terms of whose perspective it is from; they have to look at the evidence and assess its reliability; they must consider the connections between things, events and people; assess what the alternatives are, look for the underlying meaning and discuss why things matter and to whom.

There is a core curriculum which is divided into humanities and maths/sciences; teachers belong to a humanities team or a maths and science team. Instead of being divided into subjects the curriculum is organised around key questions such as 'What is justice?' 'Who is an American?' or 'Can energy disappear?' with the aim of drawing out links between subjects. Lessons are arranged in two-hour blocks. Teachers have a maximum load of forty students in any one year so that they can get to know them well. In addition to their school work all students undertake some form of community service.

The school fosters a culture of enquiry and students are encouraged to ask questions, discuss and challenge received opinion. Through discussion, the subjects which are being studied are linked back to the students' own lives. The role of the teacher is one of supporter, facilitator and coach. Staff encourage students to take responsibility for assessing, revising and expanding their work.

Assessment is based on performance rather than tests, and at the end of each year students present their work in 'exhibitions' which can consist of reports, essays, experiments, art work, drama presentations and videos. To graduate from the school students have to produce a number of portfolios in a range of subject areas and be able to discuss their work in depth with the graduation committee.

Schools within a school

Mountlake Terrace High School

The success of small schools has encouraged many large schools to look at ways of converting themselves into a number of smaller learning communities on the same site. This is a relatively recent development in America, and as the process takes a number of years there are few schools that have completed the transition. The research is therefore limited. However the interest in this whole-school reform is evidenced by a conference on this theme which took place in Seattle in Autumn 2001 and attracted around 2000 participants.

Mountlake Terrace High School, in Washington State on the West Coast, is one school which has taken this route. The process of change started with the school asking itself some fundamental questions:

- What do we want for our school?
- What is our vision of teaching and learning?
- How do we get there?
- How do we develop consensus for the development?

This dialogue led members of the school community to the recognition of the need for smaller and more personal structures. Their aim now is to create, from their large comprehensive school of 1850 students, a number of small, friendly learning communities (SLCs) where every student is known and encouraged, where teachers and students may develop productive relationships and where the quality of the teaching and learning environment is the primary concern. They are working to ensure that each small learning community is equitable and that *all* students can realise their maximum potential and become independent life-long learners.

It is the concern for all children that is driving much of this kind of reform. Schools like Mountlake Terrace High, which have looked hard at their statistics – statistics about how many children are failing and which children they are – have found that these figures themselves provide the impetus for change. To ensure a more equitable education and a more equitable society the needs of these particular children must be addressed and this can best be achieved within smaller schools where they can be known, supported and ultimately helped to succeed.

Responsibility is to be devolved from the centre and each of the small learning communities will make their own decisions concerning budget, staffing, timetabling, assessment and pedagogy. An important feature is thus to give back to teachers a real voice in the making of decisions which affect them. Moreover parents and members of the local community as well as students are to be closely involved in the design, implementation and development of each SLC. A likely outcome is that each SLC will be different and will have its own intellectual focus.

The school recognises that this is a hugely complex and lengthy process, but is convinced of the need for this kind of change. Having seen other large schools implement a range of reform programmes with varying degrees of success they have realised that scale is the critical issue.

A campus for small schools

The Julia Richman Education Complex

In 1993 the New York City Education Board closed Julia Richman, a large, failing high school and in its place, over a period of several years, established a campus of small learning communities. The campus consists of six autonomous schools, each of which has its own budget, teachers, curriculum and timetables. It also houses a crèche and play group for children of teenage parents, a health clinic, a professional development centre for teachers and an arts centre. Each of the schools has its own separate space on the campus but shares facilities such as a library, café, auditorium, pottery studio, theatre, art gallery, gym and swimming pool.

This initiative grew out of a recognition that students and teachers need a sense of belonging to a community, and that this is not possible in a large school. It gained the support of the New York Education Board which was increasingly concerned about violence in its schools. The use of scanners and security guards seemed unable to prevent young people smuggling weapons into schools and the situation in many was getting out of control. At the same time research was showing the success of many small schools in New York which were graduating a far larger proportion of their students than traditional high schools.

The Centre for Collaborative Education (the New York branch of the Coalition of Essential Schools), aware of the challenge involved in turning round a large, failing school, came up with a different solution. It proposed an experiment which entailed closing such a school and using the site to house a number of new smaller schools which children and parents could choose from. In this way they envisaged that the negative attitudes surrounding the failing school would be dispersed.

The Julia Richman School was selected as a trial and the experiment went ahead. Initially the new smaller schools were set up in different buildings in the surrounding area, whilst the large school was gradually emptied of students who had enrolled and who were allowed to graduate. This took place over a four year period. When the building was finally empty the six smaller schools, serving children from the same areas as previously served by the large school, were moved on to the campus into the original school buildings, which had been divided up to accommodate them. The schools are all very different and include a performing arts school, a school for immigrants who have only been in the country for a short while, two other high schools and an elementary school. The sixth school, the Urban Academy, is a small school which had already been in existence for some years and which was asked to go in to the project as the anchor school to provide experience.

One condition of the project was that none of the schools should have more than 300 students. The buildings are organised so that students do not have to pass through schools other than their own as they go about their business. In this way teachers know all the students that they come into contact with and vice versa. If someone is in the wrong place it is identified immediately.

To avoid competition and confrontation between the different schools some campus-wide activities are organised – for example there are athletics teams and choirs which draw students from each of the schools.

The Urban Academy, as an example of these schools, shares many of the values and practices of Central Park East Secondary School, which is described above. Classes are generally multi-aged, which is seen as a real advantage because older students can support younger students and introduce them to the culture of the school. One of the main means of learning is through discussion and seminars. Classes are often based around questions to which there are no definitive answers, and through discussion students explore their own views and come to know what their peers think. An important rule at the school is that you can attack other people's *ideas* but not attack them personally.

The hub of the school is the office in which all teachers have a desk. Students are allowed into the office and therefore see teachers working, discussing and interacting. This is seen as important, particularly for children from dysfunctional homes where such activities may be rare.

Students get to know their teachers as real people and this has a huge impact on relationships at the school.

It is clear that the Urban Academy, like the other small schools on the campus, operates very differently from a large school and it is their size that makes this possible. Their academic success – around 94 per cent of students proceed to university and do well there – is only one indicator of their achievements, all of which are attributed by staff to the effectiveness of their approach.

Looking forward

The movement towards smaller structures in education is gathering momentum across America, particularly in urban areas where the problems are greatest and where the gains seem to be the most significant. The argument in favour of economies of scale in education has been turned round and recast in terms of penalties of scale. These penalties, which include the isolation, alienation and disaffection of ever increasing numbers of young people, have massive long term social consequences and are too high a price to pay. If smaller learning communities can be shown to improve social inclusion – and the indications are that they can – the economic advantages of mass, factory schooling will fast lose their attraction. Such long term and big picture thinking is something that contemporary Britain would be foolish to ignore.

For information

Bay Area Coalition of Equitable Schools
Website: www.bayces.org

Coalition of Essential Schools
Website: www.essentialschools.org

Small Schools Project
Website: www.smallschoolsproject.org

Small Schools Workshop
Website: www.smallschoolsworkshop.org

Further reading

Ayers, W. (ed.) (2000) *A Simple Justice: The Challenge of Small Schools*, New York: Teachers College Press.

Cook, A. (1996) *Creating a Campus for Small Schools*, Bath: Human Scale Education.

Koetzsch, R. E. (1997) *The Parents Guide to Alternatives in Education*, Boston: Shambhala.

Lieberman, A. (1996) *Visit to a Small School (Trying to do big things)*, New York: NCREST.

Meier, D. (1995) *The Power of their Ideas: Lessons for America from a Small School in Harlem*, Boston: Beacon Press.

Mintz, J. (1995) *The Almanac of Education Choices*, New York: Macmillan.

Nathan, J. (1996) *Charter Schools*, San Francisco: Jossey-Bass.

Newman, R. (2000) *Building Urban Little Schools*, Cambridge, Massachusetts: Brookline.

Sizer, T. (1996) *Horace's Hope: What Works for the American High School*, Boston: Houghton Mifflin.

Chapter 12

Parents as change agents

> What the best and wisest parent wants for his own child, that must the community want for all of its children.
>
> John Dewey

Over 90 per cent of children in the UK attend traditional state schools. Many parents send their children to state schools because they support the idea of a state education system in the same way that they support the National Health Service. They believe that state schools should be good enough and available for all and that those who buy privilege for their own children are undermining the system for others. It is certainly true, perhaps in the UK more than anywhere else, that the very existence of an elitist private sector diminishes the effectiveness of the state system.

However, it is also true that many parents send their children to the local state school because they have no choice. They may not be able to afford private education, there may not be any alternative schools in their area and the option of home schooling is seen as impracticable for parents who work.

Just because parents send their children to state schools it does not mean that they are universally happy with them. Many have deep concerns but do not have anywhere to voice these concerns other than in private.

The message from the government is, of course, that our schools are improving all the time – that SATs and GCSE results are rising steadily and that negative factors are being brought under control. But this raises two questions. First – it is true that the results of able children are improving but a recent OECD report (2001) shows that whilst in most other European countries the gap between the achievers and non-achievers is narrowing, in the UK this gap is getting wider. This is a major cause for concern, for the costs and consequences for society of continuing to neglect a disaffected underclass are severe. Second, even if test and exam results are improving this does not mean that the education we are offering our children is providing them with the knowledge and skills that they need to live fulfilling and socially useful lives. Many would say that it does not. A number of employers have gone on record to express their concern that too many school leavers do not have the skills of cooperation, imagination and the ability to work independently which are required in the world of work.

For these reasons alone many schools need to change, and yet the very group who could be instrumental in bringing about positive change, namely teachers, are powerless because of the constraints – imposed by the government – within which they are operating. Indeed teacher disillusion is at an all time high and is fuelling a continuing exodus from the profession, thus threatening the sustainability of schools in their current form.

If parents want changes to the system they are going to have to press for them themselves, like the parents in the Bay Area of San Francisco who, in sheer desperation at the state of the schools in their area, have worked together to force through radical and wide ranging changes in local education provision (see Chapter 11).

In recent years there has been much talk about partnership with parents, but more often than not this means one of several things. It usually means that there is a successful Parent/Teachers Association and parents are actively involved in fund-raising for the school. It may mean that lots of parents come in and help with swimming, hearing children read or helping out in the classroom. It could mean that the turnout at parent/teacher consultations (for five or ten minutes twice a year) is high. Or it might mean that there are a few committed parent governors. Very rarely does it mean that there is an honest and ongoing dialogue between parents and the school about the values of the school, how the school is run or the way in which the education takes place there. What can parents do about this?

Most importantly, they need to make their voices heard. The Campaign for State Education (CASE) is campaigning for parent councils to be set up in all schools and at local and national levels too. Such councils could provide a structure whereby parents could be democratically consulted about education. As things stand at the moment, parent governors are supposed to represent parents' views but there is no forum in which any real consultation can take place. The existence of a parents' council would ensure that the views of parents were heard and taken seriously.

A school parents' council, made up of parent representatives from each class or tutor group, would enable parent governors to consult a representative parents' body. Such a council could meet regularly to raise and discuss issues of concern. Its views and decisions would be fed back to the school governing body through the parent governor and taken into account in school policy-making.

Each class would have its own council which could meet regularly (two or three times each year perhaps) and from which the representative for the school parents' council would be elected. In a number of other European countries such class parents' meetings form the basis of the link between home and school and provide an opportunity for many concerns to be addressed. In fact, such meetings can be a valuable means of dialogue with the class teacher or tutor on issues which concern all parents and can serve to iron out the kinds of problems which tend to arise in schools due to a lack of communication.

CASE believes that there should be a parents' council in each local education authority, consisting of parent governors from local schools to ensure that there is a body which parent governor representatives on the LEA committee could consult. Furthermore a National Parents' Council consisting of elected parent governors could represent parents' views to the government. There needs to be a channel through which the government can hear parents' concerns about education and it certainly does not exist in any formal way at the moment.

It is crucial that parents are involved in their children's education. Involved parents often become committed parents and schools benefit greatly from their support. There is considerable research to show that the education of children is most effective where parents and teachers share responsibility. It would seem however that the onus is on parents to make this partnership a reality.

There is likely to be some opposition from the teaching profession to any moves to give parents a real voice. Many teachers see this as a challenge to their professionalism and are concerned about the impact on how they operate in the classroom. The purpose of such a development, however, is to forge meaningful partnerships, based on trust, between parents and schools in an effort to loosen the chains of government control. It is only when schools have greater autonomy over their curriculum, methods of assessment and pedagogy that they will truly be able to respond to the needs of all their students. Parents have a critical role to play in pushing for such changes.

For information

Advisory Centre for Education
1B Highbury Studios
Highbury Grove
London N5 2EA
Tel: 0207 354 8321
Website: www.ace-ed.org.uk

Campaign for State Education (CASE)
158 Durham Road
London
SW20 0DG
Tel: 0208 944 8206
Website: www.casenet.org.uk

Further reading

Alexander, T. (1997) *Family Learning*, London: Demos.
Bastiani, J. and Wolfendale, S. (1996) *Home-school Work in Britain*, London: David Fulton.
Hallgarten, J. (2000) *Parents Exist, OK!?*, London: IPPR.
OECD (2001) *Education Policy Analysis*.

Conclusion

It is nothing short of a miracle that the modern methods of instruction have not yet entirely strangled the holy curiosity of enquiry; for this delicate little plant, aside from stimulation, stands mainly in need of freedom; without this it goes to wrack and ruin without fail.

Albert Einstein

The main aim of this book has been to show the range of educational alternatives available in the UK. An underlying purpose has been to question what education is about. The alternative schools and projects that are included have, for the most part, sprung from this same question. It is because their founders challenged the prevailing educational paradigm that they were established. That such a variety of schools and learning centres has been developed bears witness to the fact that there is not just one correct model but a range of ways in which children can be educated. For children are all different and consequently they learn and thrive in different environments.

A number of themes have recurred throughout the book however, indicating a broad consensus amongst these projects that children learn best when:

* The learning relates to their own life and experience
* They are encouraged to ask questions and think critically
* All aspects of their development – social, moral, emotional, creative, spiritual, physical and intellectual – are encouraged
* They are given a say in what and how they learn
* Learning takes place in a range of places, not just in the classroom
* They are known well by their teachers.

Because alternative schools have been free to experiment relatively unfettered by government orders and bureaucratic constraints, they have been able to put the interests of children at the core of their work. Teachers, parents and children have together created successful learning communities based on their own needs and aspirations. Success is not measured narrowly in terms of SATs results, but is conceived of in terms of the all-round development and achievements of the child.

There is a perception amongst some people that alternative schools are a soft option – but in the majority of cases this is far from true. Teachers assess children individually as they go along and because of their in-depth knowledge of each child are often more rigorous and more demanding than traditional schools.

These schools exist against the odds in the UK, as they currently receive no public funding whatsoever. Their challenge is twofold: not only are they working in new and innovative ways, they also have to raise all their own funds, which is no small task. The vast majority of these projects charge fees as this is the only way in which they can survive with any stability. Even so most are very under-resourced because they seek to keep fees and contributions as low as possible – but any level of fees has the unwelcome effect of making them available only to those who are able to pay. Consequently the children who would benefit most from the caring and supportive education on offer at alternative schools are denied access. Most of these schools would prefer to be publicly funded so that they could be open to all children. This is what happens in many other European countries, and in other parts of the world where more enlightened governments fund different kinds of schools in the belief that parents should be able to choose a school and an education which suits their child.

In Denmark there are hundreds of small, alternative schools and they receive around 75 per cent of their funding from the government. If a group of parents want to join together to establish a new school they can access this funding as long as there are twelve children in the first year, rising to twenty-eight in the third and subsequent years. If the figures drop below this level, the funding is removed and the school is closed. In Holland, independent schools are financed on the same basis as state schools, receiving 100 per cent of their costs from the government. As a consequence there are a significant number of Steiner, Montessori, Jenaplan and other alternative schools and these are attended by 10 per cent of all children. In Germany the situation differs from region to region, but Steiner schools have long received public funding and are thus well established as a state-funded alternative available to all parents. In America there is statutory funding for many different alternatives; in some states there are so many publicly funded alternative schools – New York for example – that there are local authority officials with responsibility for overseeing them.

All of this is a far cry from the situation in the UK. Over the past ten years successive governments have talked about diversity but this has not involved encouraging different educational approaches. Rather it has been seen in terms of redefining how state schools are funded, establishing specialist schools or encouraging private sector involvement, none of which put the interests of children to the fore. Parents can 'choose' from a range of state schools but they have to accept the government's view of what education comprises. This narrow view of diversity has had the effect of stifling real educational innovation.

As has been shown, a number of state schools are working to integrate some of the principles that underpin alternative approaches to education into their practice. This is very difficult for them within the framework that exists, where the content of learning is dictated by the National Curriculum, where children are repeatedly tested on this content and where schools are pitted against each other as a result of the league tables. Within this framework schools have very little room for manoeuvre.

There are serious problems in many of our state schools evidenced by the growing disaffection amongst young people, the rising concern of parents and the increasing frustration of teachers, many of whom are leaving the profession. Whilst the kind of education they offer may suit some children it certainly does not suit them all and too many are failing. The endemic violence, vandalism, bullying, truancy, racial intolerance and mental breakdown in many schools are indicative of the need for new ways forward. Since alternative schools both here and abroad have, in many instances, been effective both in addressing these failings and in motivating young people to learn, the arguments in favour of researching their methods, and for giving them active encouragement and financial support, are strong.

Even more importantly these schools and projects are, in many cases, educational pioneers. They are based on the values of a healthy society – of democracy, community, fairness, trust, tolerance, openness and support. Children who have experienced these values in an active way as an integral part of their education are more likely to reflect them in their own life and work. Now more than ever we are aware of the need for a new world order based on such values, and the challenge for education is thus to inculcate them. Schooling has to be more than a means of training children to contribute to economic growth regardless of the social and environmental costs.

So we need innovation and we need experiment to develop new ways of educating which respond to and shape our rapidly changing world. Education is a dynamic process and we must allow it to evolve by giving schools freedom and autonomy to respond to the challenges which they face. New projects which question outdated methods and which push at the boundaries will be instrumental in enabling society to move forward.

And there must be public funding to encourage such new and different projects. The days of a uniform and centralised education system are numbered. In a contemporary and pluralist society we need a variegated educational landscape, fully funded by the state, so that all parents are able to choose an education which suits their child. The shape of education is bound to change and schools and educational projects of the future will take many different forms. One thing is clear: we must fully embrace and encourage this change in order to equip our young people and our society for a positive future. Alternative schools offer a signpost to that future.

For further information visit www.AlternativesInEducation.co.uk

Index

A level exams 47
Aberdeen Waldorf School 61–2
Abinger Hammer Village School, Surrey 24
Accelerated Tutorial School, Birmingham 111
Acland Burghley School, Camden 163
Acorn School, Gloucestershire 52–3
adolescence: Montessori education 74–5; Steiner Waldorf education 47
Agenda 21 agreement 168–9
Alder Bridge School, Berkshire 49–50
America 3, 154–5, 175–84, 191
Ansford Community School, Somerset 169
artistic/creative development 18, 43, 105, 127
Australia 155

Babington Community Technology College, Leic. 167–8
Ball, Sir Christopher 1
Bill and Melinda Gates Foundation 177
Botton Village School, North Yorks. 59–60
Bramingham Park Study Centre, Beds. 39–40
Brighton Steiner School 50
Brockwood Park School, Hampshire 106–7

buildings 119–20
bursaries 23, 126
business: donations from 125; schools run by 161; setting up a 126

Cambridge Steiner School 56
Campaign for State Education (CASE) 186, 187-
Camphill Rudolf Steiner School, Aberdeen 69
Canada 155
Cave School, London 35–6
Cavendish First School, Yorks. 163
Central Park East School, US 178–9
Centre for Collaborative Education, New York 181–2
charities: raising funds from 121, 125; setting up of 121, 127
Charities Aid Foundation 125
Charity Commission 121
charter school movement 175–6
Christianity 102
Churchill, Winston 132
circle time 163
citizenship 89–90, 170
Coalition of Essential Schools (CES) 177, 178, 181
commercialisation 161
communities, equitable 12–14
community involvement 19, 20, 126, 129–30, 166–8
companies: setting up 121
computers in education 2, 155, 156

cooperatives 127
Cotham School, Bristol 165–6
Cotswold Chine School,
    Gloucestershire 67
Cramlington Community High
    School, Northumberland 164
creative/artistic development 18,
    43, 105, 127
curriculum 122, 127–8, 163–4;
    cross-curricular work 163–4;
    see also National Curriculum
cyber schools 155

Dame Catherine Harpur's School,
    Derbyshire 21, 33–4
decision-making 19, 89, 127, 129,
    165
democratic participation 19, 127,
    165–6, 170
democratic schools 89–98
Denmark 99, 101–2, 190
Department for Education and Skills
    (DfES) 120, 121–2
Deutsch, David 153
Dewey, John 89, 99, 100–1, 105,
    185
Dharma School, Brighton 108–9
Dog Kennel Hill Primary School,
    Southwark 163
donations 125
dyslexia/dyslexics 118

early years: Montessori education
    71–2; Reggio Emilia 99, 104–5;
    Steiner Waldorf education 44–5
Edinburgh Rudolf Steiner School
    62–4
Educare Small School, Kingston,
    Surrey 21, 25–6
Education Act (1996) 133, 153
Education Otherwise 133
Einstein, Albert 189
Elmfield Rudolf Steiner School,
    Stourbridge 57–8
emotional development 18
emotional literacy 163
environmental sustainability 12, 13,
    20, 127, 168–70
equipment and furniture 128–9

ethics 12
European Convention on Human
    Rights (1989) 133
exams *see* testing and exams

faith schools 4
fees *see under* funding
fire regulations 120
flexible schooling 150–8
Free School Movement 99, 101–2
Freinet, Célestin 99, 103–4
friendships 23, 162
funding 3, 22, 23, 101, 102, 120,
    121, 123–6, 190–1; donations
    125; fees 3, 22, 23, 48, 76, 102,
    124, 126, 190; parental voluntary
    contributions 22, 23, 125–6;
    payment in kind 23, 126
furniture and equipment 128–9

Gardner, Howard 164
GCSE exams 4, 16, 47, 128, 138,
    148
Germany 190–1
Glasgow Steiner School 64
Glen House Montessori School,
    West Yorks. 85–6
global divide 11–12
Gribble, David 95
Grundtvig, N. F. S. 99, 101–2

Hadleigh Montessori School,
    Suffolk 84
Handy, Charles 150
Harriet Costello School,
    Basingstoke 164
health and safety regulations
    120
Hearter Montessori, West Yorks.
    86–7
Her Majesty's Inspectors of Schools
    (HMI) 122
Hereford Waldorf School 59
Highbury Fields School, Islington
    163
Highfield Junior School, Plymouth
    166
holistic approach to learning 18–19,
    42, 163–4, 170

Holland 99, 102–3, 190
Holly Park Montessori School,
London 76–8
Holywood Rudolf Steiner, County
Down 61
Home School of Stoke Newington
36–7
home-based education 132–49
Human Scale Education 17–21, 22,
119, 157, 162

Ilfracombe College, Devon 168
information technology 2; *see also*
computers in education
Institut Coopératif de l'Ecole
Moderne 104
insurance 120
intellectual development 18, 43–4
Iona School, Nottingham 58
Isle of Wight Learning Zone
(IWLZ) 143–4
isolation of principle 76
Italy 99, 104–5

Jack Lobley Primary School, Essex
163
James Gillespie School, Edinburgh
166
Jenaplan schools 99, 102–3, 190
Julia Richman Education Complex,
US 181–3

kindergarten *see* early years
King Alfred's School, London
109–10
Krishnamurth, J. 106
Kumar, Satish 15, 32

Laboratory School 100
Lancaster Steiner School 60–1
Lanherne Nursery and Junior
School, Devon 83–4
league tables 9, 11, 161, 191
learning by doing 44, 72
Learning Printing Technique 103
Learning Studio, Shropshire 145
legal requirements 120, 121–2; and
flexible schooling 153; and
home-based education 133–4

Lewes New School 26–7
Little Arthur Independent School,
Isles of Scilly 28
Little London Community Primary
School, Leeds 168
local education authorities (LEAs)
124, 144, 152, 153, 154, 187
Local Exchange Trading Scheme
(LETS) 126
Lowick Primary School, Cumbria
167

magnet schools 175
Maharishi School, Lancs. 111–12
Malaguzzi, Loris 105
management structures 126–7
Meadow School, Somerset 53
Meadowbrook Montessori School,
Berkshire 79
mentoring programmes 162, 167
Michael Hall, East Sussex 50–1
Michael House Rudolf Steiner
School 59
Montessori education 71–88, 190
Montessori, Maria 71
moral choice 12
moral development 18
Moray Steiner School 64–5
motivation to learn 10, 71–2
Mountlake Terrace High School,
US 180–1
multiple intelligences, theory of
164

Nant-y-Cwm Rudolf Steiner
School, Pembrokeshire 65
National Council for Voluntary
Organisations 121
National Curriculum 2, 3, 4, 9–10,
75, 122, 124, 127, 128, 134, 150,
152, 191
National Parents' Council 187
Neill, A. S. 90
'non-essential' activities, reduction
of 10
Norfolk Lodge Nursery and
Preparatory School, Herts.
79–80
nursery education *see* early years

Oaktree Education Trust, Liverpool 40–1
Ochil Tower School, Perthshire 69
OFSTED 4, 91
Otherwise Club, London 144–5

parent councils 186–7
parental involvement 19–20, 105, 126, 129, 166–8; *see also* flexible schooling; home-based education
parental voluntary contributions 22, 23, 125–6
parents, as change agents 185–8
Park School, Dartington, Devon 21, 28–30
participation: democratic 19, 127, 165–6, 170; *see also* community involvement; parental involvement
partnerships, parental and community 19–20, 166–8
payment in kind 23, 126
peer mediation 163
Perry Court School, Kent 51
Petersen, Peter 102
Philpots Manor School, Sussex 66
physical exercise 74
Piaget, Jean 104
play 44
Potterspury Lodge School, Northants. 68
primary years: Montessori education 72–4; Steiner Waldorf education 45–6
Primrose Montessori School, London 80
Priors School, Priors Marston, Warwickshire 21, 34–5
privatisation 161
The Proletarian Educator 104
Public Educator's Cooperative 104

Raheen Wood School, County Clare 61
Rainbow Montessori School, London 80–2
Ralph Allen School, Bath 162
Readhead, Zoe 91
Reggio Emilia 99, 104–5

relationships: positive 18, 162–3, *see also* friendships
Ringwood Waldorf School, Hampshire 51
Rio Earth Summit (1992) 169
Royton and Crompton Comprehensive School, Oldham 169

St Andrew's Montessori Prep, Herts. 82
St Andrew's School, Runton, Norfolk 38–9
St Christopher's School, Bristol 67
St Christopher's School, Herts. 110
St Paul's Community Foundation School, Birmingham 40, 167
St Paul's Steiner School, London 52
salaries 123
Sands School, Devon 94–6, 97
Satellite School, London 155
Sathya Sai School, Fife 112
SATs 22, 128, 161, 185
school councils 165–6
School House, Brighton 52
School in the Woods, Freshford, Bath 30–1
Schumacher, E. F. 17
scientific method of learning 101
Scoraig Secondary School, Scotland 35
Seaford Head Community College, East Sussex 171
Self-Correcting Files 104
setting up small schools/learning centres 117–31
Sharnbrook School, Bedford 166
Sheiling School, Bristol 68
Sheiling School, Hampshire 66
Sizer, Ted 175, 177
Small Learning Communities 171, 177
Small School, Hartland, Devon 15–17, 31–3
smaller structures 21, 170–1, 175–84
South Devon Rudolf Steiner School 53–4
South London Montessori School 82–3

special educational needs (SEN)
    122, 151
special needs schools 35–41, 66–9
spiritual awareness 18–19, 44
staff 123
Stantonbury Campus, Milton
    Keynes 162, 171
state schools, alternative ways of
    working in 161–74
Steiner, Rudolf 42
Steiner Waldorf education 42–70,
    190–1
Summerhill School, Suffolk 90–4,
    98
Sunfield, Stourbridge 68–9
Sunrise Primary School, London
    110–11

teacher training, Steiner Waldorf
    education 70
teaching staff 123
technological change 1
Terrace Montessori School,
    Warwickshire 84–5
testing and exams 10–11, 128, 186;
    GCSEs 4, 47, 128, 138, 139, 148,
    185; and home-based education
    138–9, 148; SATs 128
Tolstoy, Leo 161
Towy Valley Steiner School,
    Carmarthenshire 65–6

transfers, to other schools/colleges
    23, 49, 76
trusts: operation as 121; raising
    funds from 121, 125

unincorporated associations 121
Urban Academy 182–3

virtual schools 155
Vygotsky, L. 105

Waldorf College Project,
    Gloucestershire 54
'walking buses' 170
Weobley School, Hertfordshire.
    169–70
West Walker Primary School,
    Newcastle 167
Wharfedale Montessori School and
    College, North Yorks. 87
Willow House, Sutton 27
Willow Tree Montessori School,
    Crawley 83
Wolf, Kolya 153
Wolsey Junior School, South
    London 170
Wynstones School, Gloucester 55–6

York Steiner School 60
Young (of Dartington), Michael
    Young, Lord 99